GAMES
Magazine Presents

Best Pencil Puzzles

EDITED BY WILL SHORTZ

Random House
Puzzles & Games

All of the puzzles that appear in this work were originally published in
Games Magazine.

ISBN 0-8129-2080-5

Manufactured in the United States of America

22 21 20 19 18 17 16

CONTENTS

CONTENTS

INTRODUCTION

"The great source of pleasure is variety," wrote Samuel Johnson. "Variety is the mother of enjoyment," penned Benjamin Disraeli. "Variety's the very spice of life," concurred William Cowper.

In compiling this collection of the best pencil puzzles from GAMES Magazine, we've followed the wisdom of the above literary giants and included lots of variety. In particular, we've selected samples of regular variety puzzles that are the most popular with GAMES's readers. These include double-crostics, Pencil Pointers, crisscrosses, word searches, diagramlesses, logic problems, cryptograms, Crypto-Funnies, and assorted novelty puzzles that are difficult to classify (and sometimes even to duplicate!). There are even crosswords to add variety to the variety.

Because of the varied contents of this book and the way it is formatted, you'll never know exactly what kind of challenge awaits you on the next page. Anticipation is part of the fun, as well as the different ways in which your brain gets twisted and massaged.

As always, I'd like to give special acknowledgment to Mike Shenk, who was the original editor of many of the puzzles in the book. I'd like to thank Amy Goldstein for her diligence and care in preparing the manuscript; Robert Altemus for expertly redesigning the material for book form; and all the editors and artists at GAMES over the years who polished the puzzles before their first appearance in print.

Now, to quote Plato: "The beginning is the most important part of the work." So turn the page and dig in!

Will Shortz

PATHFINDER

You'll need to think straight to twist your way through this variety crossword. Most answers take a winding path through the grid, making one or more right-angle turns. (One answer is entered straight.) The letter after each clue number indicates the answer's starting direction (north, south, east, or west), and the number in parentheses after the clue indicates the length of the answer. Each letter in the completed grid will appear in exactly two words—no more, no less. *ANSWER, PAGE 114*

CLUES

1W House for a Honda (6)

2W Bandleader Shaw (5)

3E Kind of Court or Being (7)

4W Relative of a thumbtack (7)

5S *Jungle Book*'s Shere Khan (5)

6S 2.54 centimeters (4)

7S Coffee and chocolate blend (5)

8E Brief news item (9)

8S Sleepwear (7)

9W Pop's partner (3)

10S Antipasto ingredient (6)

11S Not entirely open (4)

12S Look for (4)

13W Voice an objection (8)

14N Light show equipment (5)

15S Yucatan Indian (4)

16N Like some twins (7)

17N Constructed (4)

18S Two cents' worth (3)

19W Capture, as in chess (4)

20S Miss Redgrave (7)

21S Kaddafi's country (5)

22N Thundershower or hurricane (5)

22S Bobby or Boston Red (3)

23S Outcome (6)

24S Backyard cookout (8)

25W Unctuous (4)

26N Sextant operator (9)

27N San Diego or Bronx attraction (3)

27S Horse of different colors? (5)

28N Put forth energy (5)

29N Exploiter (4)

30E Pirate's sword (7)

BEEP! BEEP!

ANSWER, PAGE 114

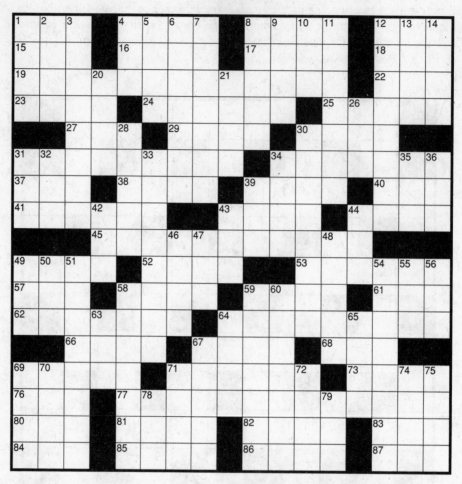

ACROSS

1 "What'd you say?"
4 Retirement accounts: Abbr.
8 Close with a bang
12 ___ constrictor
15 Soldier's address: Abbr.
16 Actress D'Orsay
17 Tennis star Mandlikova
18 Fanciful vase
19 Cornucopias: 3 wds.
22 Young fellow
23 ___ Karenina
24 African desert
25 Add up the score
27 Abbreviation in business names
29 Little bit
30 Poet Ogden
31 "Stormy Weather" singer: 2 wds.
34 Chicken breed
37 Gold: Sp.
38 Folksinger Burl
39 Hardens, as a mold
40 Fish eggs
41 Dennis the ___
43 Hammer or hacksaw
44 Skier's "powder"
45 Swindle
49 Swedish pop group
52 Comedian Jay
53 Sorcerer-like
57 Twice XXVI
58 Chilly
59 1974 Gould-Sutherland film
61 "___ You Lonesome Tonight?" (Presley hit)
62 Mariner's warning sound
64 Sailor's dances
66 Clasped
67 Sandy hill
68 Sault ___ Marie
69 "Saw wood" while sleeping
71 Built ___ (well-constructed): 2 wds.
73 Cartoonist Addams, for short
76 Balloon contents
77 Noted Alp or a Disneyland ride: 2 wds.
80 Tavern
81 Melody
82 Top rating
83 Genetic stuff
84 Broadway hit ___ Misérables
85 Finishes
86 Haughty one
87 Eggy drink

DOWN

1 Joke response
2 "Once ___ a time ..."
3 Intrude: 3 wds.
4 No ___, ands, or buts
5 Grande and Lobo
6 ___ de coeur (amour)
7 Gas-stealing tubes
8 He-Man's female counterpart
9 Actress Turner
10 Picnic pest
11 Kenmore rivals
12 Attention-getter in a crowd
13 By mouth
14 Amos's radio sidekick
20 Zola novel
21 Tardy
26 Barbecue leftover
28 One of the Marx Brothers
30 Famous English actress of the 1600s: 2 wds.
31 Actor Herbert
32 "Able was I ___ I saw Elba"
33 Operation ___ (D-Day codename)
34 Topper star ___ Carroll: 2 wds.
35 Australian hopper, for short
36 Original
39 Sticky gunk
42 Eureka!
43 Couple
44 Collector's goal
46 Advertising light
47 "Live from New York" show: Abbr.
48 Has a speech impediment
49 TV alien
50 Life story, for short
51 Wild sheep
54 Tip of South America: 2 wds.
55 Old empire of Europe: Abbr.
56 "You bet!"
58 Gigi author
59 Musical pieces
60 Sergeant ___ of the Yukon
63 That woman
64 Waikiki dance
65 Have poison ivy
67 Rotunda tops
69 Go boating
70 Three squared
71 Care for
72 "... a ___'clock scholar": 2 wds.
74 Italian river
75 Hosiery problem
78 Attila the ___
79 Yank's foe

CRYPTO-FUNNIES 1

In this comic strip, all the dialogue has been converted into a cryptogram. That is, every letter of the alphabet has been consistently substituted by another letter throughout the cartoon. For example, if G represents V in one word, it will represent V in every word. Look for distinctive letter patterns and punctuation to help you get started. *ANSWER, PAGE 114*

1.

2.

3.

4.

WHAT'S ON TAP?

As the plumber might say, if a leaky spigot doesn't close, don't faucet. The same might be said for a pun that doesn't quite work—but we've never let that stop us! The puzzle is to find the 36 plumbing terms listed at the bottom of the page in the letters of the leaky faucet below. Each reads horizontally, vertically, or diagonally, but always in a straight line. We think you'll find solving a lead-pipe cinch; but if not, you'll find all the answers on tap on page 114.

```
    T A L        K I N G          I S E
  F A E V L A V F F O T U H S H Y D R K A
  F L A R E F I T T I N G P B U T H T A B
  N T U P I P E T H R E A D E R I N T N H
    E Y X          E N              A R S
                   N D
                   E A A N
                 R D E W R J
                 I T L F O I
                 N C I G
                 N X
    I S E A R F A T I T O G I P S U R
  S T O P P E R C S S A U E B O I L E R E T U
  H P S I T V E A E I R R R S C S E G N A L F I N T H
  E C H P O I A U A S E O D E P E U N N I D N G T H E F
  I R W R R M S L I P N U T S I S U A E P I P N I A R D
T S O L D E R I N G I R O N R E L I E F V A L V E T O A
K L T W R E N E H C N E R W E P I P E C U T T E R S U S
  F F A E L H G                    L T O H E E P T R
  L E R N S T                      R S S P U E R
E U C O A A                          F F I R T
H S R W P E                            S P E
C H O E O
O P S N R
D I S B P
Y R P V O B E
R T E A F R O
    L
    L V
  S E T
  T R O
E A D I I
P M A L C
T H R E U
  D Y T
```

BATHTUB

BOILER

CLAMP

CROSS VALVE

DRAIN CLEANER

DRAIN PIPE

FAUCET

FIXTURES

FLANGES

FLARE FITTING

FLOW PIPE

FLUSH PIPE

FLUX

JOINT-SEALING TAPE

PIPE CUTTERS

PIPE TAP

PIPE THREADER

PIPE WRENCH

PLIERS

PLUNGER

PROPANE TORCH

RADIATOR

REAMER

RELIEF VALVE

ROUTER

SCREWDRIVER

SHUTOFF VALVE

SLIP NUTS

SNAKE

SOLDERING IRON

SPANNER

SPIGOT

STOPPER

TOILET

TRAP

WASHERS

PENCIL POINTERS 1

In this crossword the clues appear in the grid itself. Enter the answers in the direction of the pointers.

ANSWER, PAGE 114

The crossword grid contains the following clues:

- Popular Yule carol
- The __ Ranger
- Sign of the future
- Sentry's "stop!"
- Black leopard
- They sit on saucers
- Leave out
- Start
- Jane Eyre author
- One who guffaws
- Karate skill level markers
- A __ of Two Cities
- Martini garnish
- Frisco NFLer, for short
- Beauty pageant dress
- Touch, sight, or smell
- "Hi," in Honolulu
- Paving for old streets
- MCMXC, for example
- __ and kicking
- Prepared for prayer
- Gorge oneself, slangily
- Table-cloth material
- Agent's fraction
- Wounds inflicted by bees
- Makes smooth
- Message sent by wire
- Lured, as by flirting
- "Bald" bird
- Say "hi" to
- Place for a sacrifice
- Cash, in slang
- To the __ degree
- Animals' dens
- Title for a knight
- One of the Great Lakes
- Talked a lot, but said little
- Snake-like fishes
- __ Angeles
- Totally silly
- Title giver
- Chairs
- Listen to
- Yule fireplace item
- Ireland's capital
- Supports beside stairs
- Border
- Frog's cousin
- 1,000-year periods
- Time of early tools
- Actor's part
- Book to keep photos in
- Race-track tipster
- Pacific island group
- __ foot (lucky charm)
- Ocean-landing vehicle
- Sala-mander
- Psycho actress Leigh
- Banish
- Metric "quart"
- Small cities
- French friend
- Phone answer word
- Rear ends of boats
- River mouth feature
- ERA or RBI
- Water down
- Make a knot in
- Healthy cereal choice
- Roof overhang
- T-bone cutting utensil
- Peevish
- State-ments of truth
- Carved whale-bone
- Tennis court need
- Optimally
- Silly asses
- Placed in a secret spot
- "Eureka!"
- School of whales
- Captain Hook, for one
- Valley
- Sore
- They fall in the fall
- __ by (honored a ruling)
- Tidy
- Unim-portant facts
- Draft drinks
- Photo-copier powder
- Informed
- Search (into books)
- Loafed around
- His job is brain-storming
- Entire range
- Pie in the __
- Bowl Game setting
- Church area
- Rotten kid
- Implore
- Lots of
- CHiPs actor Estrada
- "One of these __"
- Planted
- Highbrow fellow
- Summer, in France
- Add a change
- Every-thing included
- Loathing
- Niña, Pinta, & Santa __
- Gall
- Fly a jet or a glider
- Combine into one
- Avarice
- Made moist
- Little tots

AWARDS NIGHT

Fill in these 44 words and phrases relating to award ceremonies so that they interlock in standard crisscross fashion in the grid. When the puzzle is completed, each word will be used exactly once.

ANSWER, PAGE 115

4 LETTERS
FILM
HOST
LIMO
LIVE
SKIT
TONY
TOUT

5 LETTERS
ALBUM
CLIOS
EDGAR

EMMYS
HONOR
OBIES
OSCAR
PRIZE

6 LETTERS
ANNUAL
BALLOT
CINEMA
MOVIES
TROPHY
YEARLY

7 LETTERS
ACTRESS
VICTORY

8 LETTERS
AUDIENCE
DIRECTOR
NOMINEES
SUSPENSE

9 LETTERS
ANNOUNCER
SOAP OPERA

STATUETTE
"YOU LIKE ME!"

10 LETTERS
ACCEPTANCE
SUPPORTING

11 LETTERS
BEST PICTURE
COMMERCIALS
"THE WINNER IS ..."

12 LETTERS
ACADEMY AWARD

COUNTRY MUSIC
GOLDEN GLOBES

13 LETTERS
BEST NEW ARTIST
"I'D LIKE TO THANK ..."
SONG OF THE YEAR

14 LETTERS
OPENING NUMBERS
SEALED ENVELOPE

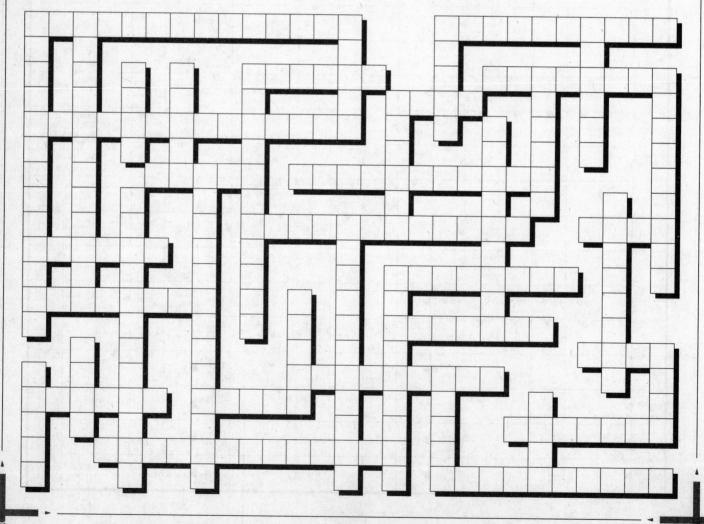

DOUBLE CROSS 1

Answer the clues for words to be entered on the numbered dashes. Then transfer the letters on the dashes to the correspondingly numbered squares in the puzzle grid to spell a quotation reading from left to right. Black squares separate words in the quotation. Work back and forth between grid and word list to complete the puzzle. When you are done, the initial letters of the words in the word list will spell the author's name and the source of the quotation.

ANSWER, PAGE 115

1L	2G	3F	4D	5E	6T		7O	8U		9S	10T		11J	12L	13I		14P	15H	16U	17C	18A	19J	20K
	21S	22A	23E	24L		25N	26O	27P	28R		29F		30N	31L	32T	33H	34O	35P		36A	37U	38Q	39C
40T	41L	42M	43K	44B		45D	46N		47P		48I	49U	50G	51C	52E		53J	54B	55H	56O		57F	58D
59L	60S		61G	62I	63U		64B	65Q	66L	67D	68O		69I	70D	71S	72N	73P		74T	75Q		76N	77O
78C	79M		80Q	81D	82C	83P	84H	85O	86I		87A	88D		89T	90S	91H		92Q	93C	94U	95M	96P	97I
98D	99J		100Q	101O		102G	103A	104B		105P	106Q	107J	108K	109R		110F	111U	112H	113D	114L	115N		116T
117S	118D		119H	120J	121D	122A	123F	124R		125S	126O		127L	128G	129B		130T	131I	132N	133J	134B		135B
136S	137T		138R	139A	140L	141B		142N	143E	144A	145I		146C	147K		148L	149A	150E		151J	152I	153Q	154G
	155C	156L		157G	158H	159C		160H	161U	162G	163Q	164J	165A	166N		167I	168K	169D		170A	171K	172H	173F
174U		175U	176M	177N	178S	179L	180A	181B	182J		183B	184L		185G	186O	187D	188A	189Q	190S		191O	192H	193P

A. 1600 Pennsylvania Ave. (3 wds.)
 18 22 36 87 103 180 122 149 139
 165 188 170 144

B. Gnu
 183 54 181 44 134 135 129 104 64 141

C. Child's weekly stipend
 17 39 93 78 146 155 51 82 159

D. Best Picture of 1934 (with "E") (3 wds.)
 4 45 58 113 67 70 118 121 88
 169 187 98 81

E. See Clue "D"
 5 23 52 143 150

F. Be of importance
 3 29 57 110 123 173

G. Extended, as one's arms
 2 50 61 102 128 154 162 185 157

H. Star of *One Million Years B.C.* (2 wds.)
 55 172 15 84 160 33 112 91 192
 119 158

I. Former pro basketballer "The Big 'E'" (2 wds.)
 13 131 152 97 145 62 167 48 86 69

J. Anchor for a wall hanging (2 wds.)
 11 19 53 99 107 120 133 151 182 164

K. University officer
 20 43 108 147 168 171

L. First Lady of Mystery (2 wds.)
 31 148 59 127 179 140 1 12 114
 66 24 156 41 184

M. A.M., poetically
 95 176 79 42

N. Sight of delight for a skier (2 wds.)
 76 132 177 115 72 166 30 25 46 142

O. 1962 Katherine Anne Porter novel (3 wds.)
 85 186 7 101 77 191 126 34 26
 56 68

P. Beatles album featuring "Here Comes The Sun" (2 wds.)
 83 96 105 14 193 35 27 47 73

Q. Alexander the Great's steed
 80 106 92 153 38 65 163 189 100 75

R. It's usually due on the 1st
 124 109 28 138

S. Breed of English dog used in water hunting
 9 21 60 71 90 117 125 136 178 190

T. Stirring things up
 89 6 74 137 40 116 32 10 130

U. "The Man of La Mancha" (2 wds.)
 175 111 8 161 16 94 37 49 174 63

BY LOU KESTEN

Classified Chaos

Each of the people on these two pages is thinking of making a career change, and, to that end, each has applied for one of the jobs circled in the classified ads at right. Unfortunately, each of them had the wrong idea of what the job entailed. For example, the filmmaker who had worked with Art Carney (#1) thought he might be qualified for the ART DIRECTOR position. Can you match each of these characters to the job that he or she mistakenly applied for?

ANSWERS, PAGE 114

10

11

12

13

14

15

STEVE MELLOR

INTERNAL LOGIC

ANSWER, PAGE 115

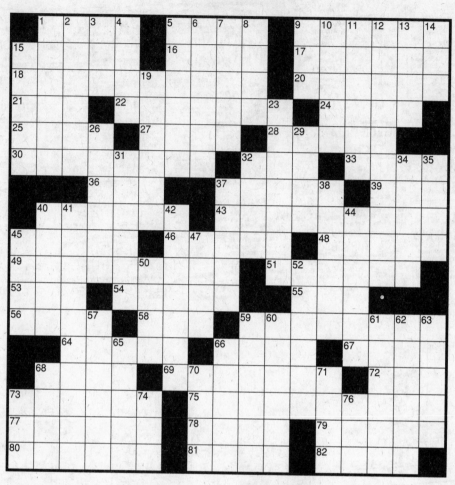

ACROSS

1 "I couldn't ___ less!"
5 Avoid scrupulously
9 He enjoys being cruel
15 Bright-colored eel
16 ___ avail (uselessly): 2 wds.
17 Tree-lined street
18 Likely to happen: 3 wds.
20 Elevated
21 Friend in France
22 More apologetic
24 Oohs and ___
25 Ship's pole
27 Enthusiastic
28 Part of a pound
30 Losing money: 3 wds.
32 "___, humbug!"
33 Declines, as the tide
36 Burro
37 Baseball cap part
39 Mauna ___ (Hawaiian volcano)
40 Seedless, as prunes
43 Uninformed: 3 wds.
45 Short-beaked songbird
46 Fat
48 Sneaker fasteners
49 Informed: 3 wds.
51 Bar orders
53 Expression from a moron
54 Moreno and Coolidge
55 "Do ___ say" ("Obey me"): 2 wds.
56 World oil cartel, for short
58 City trains
59 Naked: 3 wds.
64 Purple shade
66 Pesky insect
67 Crippled
68 Army barracks beds
69 Molasses, in Britain
72 Actor Beatty, of *Superman*
73 February and March, e.g.
75 Mistaken: 3 wds.
77 Egg dish
78 Con ___ (spiritedly, in music)
79 ___ cologne (perfume): 2 wds.
80 Check writers
81 Envisions
82 Goes down, as the sun

DOWN

1 Swindler: 2 wds.
2 Painter or sculptor
3 Cheering word
4 The holes in needles
5 Go without food
6 Absolutely dreadful
7 Took apart
8 Schnozzola
9 Actor Mineo
10 Of birds
11 Make unreadable, as a coin
12 Profitable: 3 wds.
13 Takes to court
14 TV tycoon Turner
15 Home of the Dolphins
19 Crude and vulgar
23 Heated, as peanuts
26 Make straw roofs
29 "I'm in trouble now!"
31 Swimming actress Williams
32 Coal storage places
34 Ho-hum people
35 Fashionable New York store
37 Vistas
38 Pickled hot dog topping
40 Sex symbol's poster
41 Rich: 3 wds.
42 "___ the Sun Go Down on Me" (Elton John song): 2 wds.
44 Fellow in the lion's den
45 Traditional dog's name
47 "Constrictive" snakes
50 Capital of Ukraine
52 "Shake, ___ & Roll"
57 Cows, steers, oxen, etc.
59 How some games end: 3 wds.
60 Mexican snack chips dish
61 Expired, as a subscription: 2 wds.
62 Changes the Constitution
63 Pie slice shape
65 Theater worker
66 Literary category
68 Unconscious state
70 Chest bones
71 Lambs' mothers
73 Swabbing need
74 Holy men: Abbr.
76 *Norma* ___

QUOTE BOXES

To solve Quote Boxes, drop the letters from each vertical column—not necessarily in the order in which they appear—into the empty squares below them to spell a quotation reading from left to right, line by line. Black squares indicate ends of words. A word not stopped at the end of one line is continued on the next. The source of each quote is given above the grid.

ANSWERS, PAGE 115

1. ELLEN BARKIN

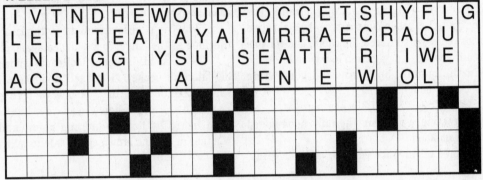

2. CHARLES KURALT

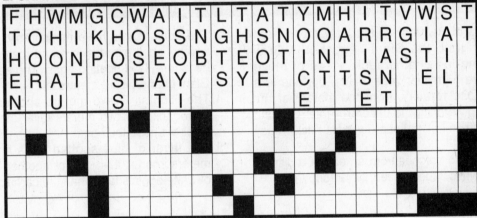

WORD LADDERS

The object of a Word Ladder is to turn one word into another by changing one letter at a time, making a common, uncapitalized English word each step of the way. No letters should be scrambled from one step to the next. For example, to change WARM into COLD in four steps, you could write WARM, WARD, WORD, CORD, COLD. How many of the four meat-related Word Ladders below can you complete in the number of steps listed?

ANSWERS, PAGE 115

1. PORK (4 steps) **2. MEAT** (4 steps) **3. WISH** (5 steps) **4. BEEF** (6 steps)

CHOP   LOAF   BONE   HASH

BY EMILY COX & HENRY RATHVON

GREAT EGGS-PECKED-ATIONS

The frantic distress signal pulsing across space from Dr. Rex Allison's one-man research outpost on the planet Redfern was received by the Cavalry, a patrol craft. But the rescue ship was too late to save Dr. Allison from whatever calamity had befallen him.

Rescue patrolmen Rugg and McReady strode into Dr. Allison's research station with blast pistols in hand. The doctor was gone, and the place was a wreck. Smashed equipment and scattered papers littered the cabin, and terrible claw marks scarred the walls. Rugg gave a low whistle. As he kicked around in the rubble, he uncovered something unexpected—a knee-high, mud brown egg.

"Look at that," said Rugg. "It's still incubating."

Indeed it was—resting warmly in the only undamaged mechanical nest that remained.

"I suppose we should take it back with us," said McReady.

"It's all that's left of the poor guy's work."

"Wait one minute," barked Rugg, rummaging among the papers on the floor. "Get a load of these notes."

The patrolmen bent to peruse the disconnected jottings, and as they did so, they heard in the distance, muffled by the jungles of Redfern, the roar of some enormous animal. It made them read more hastily.

"Why can't these scientists write plainly?" groaned Rugg, flinching as the jungle roar sounded again, closer this time.

"Never mind," snapped McReady, jamming the papers into his jumpsuit pocket. "I can tell from these notes whether it's safe to take the egg. And by the way—let's get going!"

With the notes below, can you, like McReady, identify each lizard by height and egg color, and thus determine whether or not the brown egg is safe to take along?

ANSWER, PAGE 114

DR. ALLISON'S NOTES

1. The big lizards of Redfern are four in number. I call them the Ringtail, the Giant Leaper, the Gray Plateback, and the Leatherneck. Three of these behemoths are harmless vegetarians, but one is a carnivore whose ferocity, from the instant of the brute's sudden hatching, is uncontrollable. On field trips I must remember to keep my blast rifle in easy reach.

2. Each type of lizard hatches from an egg of a distinct color: brown, white, blue-spotted, or red-spotted.

3. The adult lizards have measurably different heights, which I shall express in round meters. The tallest, a herbivore, lays spotted eggs. The second tallest, the Giant Leaper, is 12 meters tall.

4. The Ringtail is two meters shorter than the Gray Plateback and two meters taller than a herbivorous layer of unspotted eggs.

5. The layer of blue-spotted eggs has a height two meters shorter than that of another lizard. The layer of white eggs is taller than the carnivore.

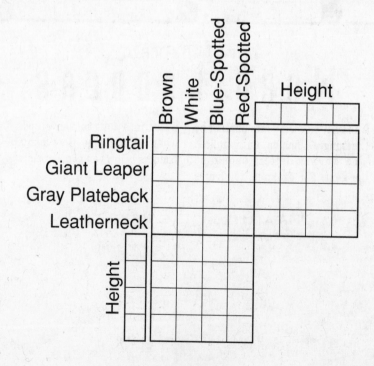

WACKY WORDIES

Over the years, GAMES has run many pages of Wacky Wordies, usually promising each one would absolutely, positively be our last—until we'd break down due to popular demand and print more a few issues later. We continue here in this great tradition, now in book form. As always, the game is to discover the familiar word, phrase, or saying represented by each arrangement of letters. For example, #1 below depicts "Leave no stone unturned."

ANSWERS, PAGE 116

1. STONE STONE STONE STONE STONE STONE STONE	**2.** DOft.OR	**3.** GO ――――――― Jan. 6 Jan. 6	**4.** GREENNV
5. LOOK ME E Y E	**6.** PROMISE	**7.** L C L U U R P B	**8.** QQ ME
9. A+ PERFORM NCE	**10.** TAKE ――――― JOB	**11.** 8 − 6 = 2	**12.** NOW^{HE}RE
13. 21 lb. 18 lb. HAND FOOT	**14.** SUIT SIT IT T	**15.** KNOW IT TI	**16.** HIS.TORY

17.
 	
LAWYER
	18.
	
	       T E
	          G
	BED G
		19.
		
		VIRGO
		....
			20.
			
			C O D U C T
			  N

FROM THE BOOK WORDoodles BY MARVIN MILLER

BY HELEN TAYLOR

TEXAS LEAGUER

Here's a Texas-sized word search in honor of the Lone Star State. The 36 words and phrases are hidden deep in the heart of the Texas grid, reading vertically, horizontally, or diagonally, but always in a straight line. If the task is too big for you, you'll find the answer on page 115.

```
                    J T E X A S
                    R O C A W I
                    E S L S A S
                    W T L L A T
                    I A I T I N
                    N E B U O R J F
                    G M S I Q U A A S T R O D O M E N D T
                    E X O A D S T M C R A N C H E S B S A
                    I H C G S A E N A I O B S S I A L E N
                    S T E S I O X M N A N R N B W M U O A
                    V R P E A R A E L R E T R L O H E P K T
S L L E W L I O O O E R E X S A L L I S O E B O B A R T
    I S A N A A Y E W B V A A O T I P I O H S M U O N A O
    N I N R B E V T I I E I U O R Y A S G O I S N H X E
      N T E X A S R A N G E R S S E S S N R J T N A E O
      F A D T H D O E T W B T I T O O A O W A O E N T R
      N D O F E R F O N S M E T E I I H L O L N T D E B
      O O R K T     R O R X N A D N V E L E L D L S
      W I           T T A H D C O M A L A H A E
                    C S T R L T G I E E D
   ABILENE          J. R. EWING       A E S Y N B S Y B
   ALAMO            JUDGE ROY BEAN     Y C V E A J O
   AMARILLO         LAREDO             H T L N N
   ASTRODOME        LONE STAR STATE      S U A O
   AUSTIN           LONGHORNS            T E S G L
   BIG BEND         MESQUITE             I N B E
   BLUEBONNET       OILERS               C K
   CACTUS           OIL WELLS
```

ABILENE	J. R. EWING		
ALAMO	JUDGE ROY BEAN		
AMARILLO	LAREDO		
ASTRODOME	LONE STAR STATE		
AUSTIN	LONGHORNS		
BIG BEND	MESQUITE		
BLUEBONNET	OILERS		
CACTUS	OIL WELLS		
DALLAS	PANHANDLE	RIO GRANDE	TEXARKANA
EL PASO	PECOS BILL	SAM HOUSTON	TEXAS OUR TEXAS
FORT WORTH	PRAIRIE DOGS	SAN ANTONIO	TEXAS RANGERS
GALVESTON	RANCHES	SAN JACINTO	WACO
JIM BOWIE	RED RIVER	TEN-GALLON HAT	YELLOW ROSE

PENCIL POINTERS 2

In this crossword the clues appear in the grid itself. Enter the answers in the direction of the pointers.

ANSWER, PAGE 116

Tie up / Chatter foolishly	▼	Real soon, in memos	Dialer's book	Adam's home	Nipper was their mascot	▼	Metal-yielding rock	H.S. math course	*Animal House* festivity	Narrow groove	Europe's "boot"	▼	*Barney Miller*'s Linden	Road curve	Writers' aliases	▼	Central Texas city	PG-13 and R
					Layers of paint	▼					1989 ursine movie							▼
Place to buy a lemon?											__ in "apple" Rank	▼			The Celtics' org.		
Auction					Hoover, for one	Chinese menu items	▼								Word with wit or pick		
Use up, as money				▼		Football official	Castle in France	Light and fluffy	▼				Film *The Barefoot __*	Burden	Actress MacGraw		
St. Louis landmark	Bus rider Parks	Place for a goatee		Circle part				Tablet Fork feature				Swindlers	▼				
			Baton wielder Zubin							British prep school					U.K. language Rue	▼		
Finder's cry	▼		Flock females	More light-skinned	▼						Hospital workers	▼					
Tendon				Blasting stuff Pigpen	▼			Houston footballer	Perfect place	Mao __-tung					Trip around a track	Common makeup item	Ending for Siam or Japan
Freshly				"__ later, alligator"						Turkish ruler		__ club (singing group)	▼				
Gagarin and Andropov	Addict	Gamma's follower / Irritate	▼				__ *États-Unis*	Play __ it lays / TV's Ron	▼			Beams of light	▼				
	▼			Xmas fireplace burners								Fencing weapon	▼				
Knight's address	▼		Compete (with)	Mileage rating org.	Ping-pong need	Babar, for one	▼						▼	Wicked		Like "recieve"
Natural roll in craps						Neighbor of Lebanon	▼				Begin to enjoy, as a hobby	Precise	Energy Boxer Tyson	▼		
Cook-book offering						What "&" means	Billy goat feature	The __ of the land	Greek vowel		Zodiac twins					
Treaty org.	*One Day __ Time*	Place to sip Tetley Crag								Doing well, in games	Banishes	▼				
▼			Of the lower spine	Hooked up to the computer	"Nifty!"	▼					Greedy ones	▼				
Trunk of the body					Israel's Moshe __						Rink material Keys			Not long-distance	Fill with joy
Of Nordic stock	▼				Andy Taylor's son	"Born in the __"		"Brewski"	__ *Mis-behavin'* / Cal. sch.	▼			Grant foe Italian money	▼	
Self-centered activities	__ long way (stretch)	Month after Sept.	Storm Vietnam holiday	▼								Laze / Dem.'s rivals	▼		
▼						Of the environ-ment	▼								
Pacific land group						French fashion magazine					Speak in public				
British leader Clement					Some language tests	▼					Lost color	▼			

ANSWER, PAGE 116

ACROSS

1 Pork sources
5 Collected
12 Cannon's sound
16 Not working
17 Snail-shaped ear canal
18 Civil liberties group: Abbr.
19 Fly like an eagle
20 Chuck wagon cook's command: 4 wds.
22 Miles Standish's rival John
24 Madonna's ex Penn
25 Appreciative opera cry
26 Lymph mass
28 Snoopy and Marmaduke, e.g.
31 Diarist Anaïs
32 "All ___!" (conductor's cry)
35 Over yonder
37 By the ___ of one's pants
38 Antony's command: 4 wds.
41 Away from the wind
42 Furnish with weapons
43 Understood
47 Actress Farrow
48 What Tarzan swings on
50 Miss America's ribbon
51 "___ Maria"
52 Hitting, as with a strap
54 "The lowest form of humor"
55 *The Iliad,* e.g.
56 Ray Charles's command: 4 wds.
60 Bird of ___ (falcon, e.g.)
63 Atmospheric layer
64 Gets by force
65 Slippery fish
66 Astounds
67 Actor Guinness
68 Fend off
70 Hammer or screwdriver
73 Afflicted with poison ivy
77 Elvis's command: 3 wds.
81 Butter substitute
82 ___ out (makes ends meet)
83 Put back in good repair
84 Depend (upon)
85 Parking garage mishap
86 Club Med sites
87 Song for one

DOWN

1 Leaning Tower's city
2 False god
3 Pleased
4 Sing a love song to
5 Duke or UNC's sports conference: Abbr.
6 Bullwinkle, for one
7 Mountain's peak
8 Mets' stadium
9 Defame
10 Poetic adverb
11 Papa
12 1930s heavyweight champ Max
13 Gas rating number
14 Singer Newton-John
15 *Teenage ___ Ninja Turtles*
21 *Pygmalion* author's monogram
23 Comedian Crosby
27 JFK's predecessor
29 Spaghetti sauce spice
30 First and reverse, for two
32 Gentle as ___: 2 wds.
33 Misrepresent
34 *Love Story* star Ryan
35 Ripped
36 "... can you ___ a few bars?"
37 Old draft org.: Abbr.
39 China's longest river
40 Cheerleader's cry
44 The Mamas and the ___
45 Kick out of an apartment
46 Ships' floors
48 7 on a sundial
49 Being dragged, as a car: 2 wds.
50 Certain
53 Your, in the Bible
54 Pigsty
55 Pilots' seats, in emergencies
57 Twinkie maker
58 Cobbler's instrument
59 Three: Ger.
60 Rang, as a bell
61 Declare void, as a license
62 Almost a dozen
66 24-hour banking convenience, for short
67 On one's toes
69 Take five
71 Aware of
72 Bad smell
74 Egyptian queen, informally
75 Satan's realm
76 Toy that "walks the dog"
78 Blunder
79 Golf peg
80 Thing, in law

DOUBLE CROSS 2

Directions appear on page 15.

ANSWER, PAGE 116

1P	2T		3B	4V	5A	6F	7M	8W	9S		10H	11I		12T	13C		14Q	15A	16F		17T	18I	19H	20X
21P	22D	23U		24J	25T		26A	27F	28X	29S	30D	31K		32H	33V	34W	35Q	36R	37L	38A	39I	40E		41O
42D	43T	44P	45B	46V	47F	48Y	49H	50N	51I		52R	53L		54T	55O	56Y		57Q	58D		59N	60F	61M	62T
	63K	64J	65X	66I	67R	68B	69E	70T		71P	72H	73U	74A		75M	76N	77I	78O		79E	80N	81C		82S
83A	84F		85H	86D	87K		88Q	89S	90I	91O		92U	93X	94R	95F		96L	97H	98O		99M	100K	101S	
102G	103V	104E	105U		106O	107P	108H		109I	110Y	111T	112U	113B		114N	115Y		116W	117K		118T		119J	120F
121V	122U	—	123W	124J	125M	126G	127R	128P	129C		130N	131U	132Q		133L	134T	135D	136X	137W	138K	139U		140G	141O
142B	143S		144H	145W		146Q	147C	148U	149O	150L	151I	152N	153Y	154G	155K	156P		157U	158H	159X	160B	161M	162T	
163Q		164N	165P	166I		167G	168K	169O	170X	171U	172B		173S	174N	175R		176Q	177O		178M	179F		180D	
181J	182I	183U	184W	185R	186O	187X	188G	189B		190V	191X	192J	193H	194L	195W	196R								

A. Foe of the Green Knight, in Arthurian legend
5 15 74 26 38 83

B. *The Meaning of Relativity* author
113 142 160 172 189 3 45 68

C. Information on a racetrack tote board
81 129 147 13

D. Seven-time AL batting champ (2 wds.)
30 42 166 135 180 22 58 86

E. Gangster's guns
40 69 79 104

F. Automotive heir who had a lemon named after him (2 wds.)
120 16 27 47 6 179 60 95 84

G. Lamb stew meat
102 126 140 154 167 188

H. Smithsonian, for one
10 19 32 49 72 85 97 108 144 158 193

I. Midwestern metropolis where "everything's up to date" (2 wds.)
90 18 39 66 77 109 151 182 11 51

J. Corrects copy
64 181 192 24 119

K. Cuspidor
138 63 155 168 31 87 100 117

L. Tolkien creatures
37 150 96 133 194 53 124

M. What guests sometimes do with their welcome
178 61 75 125 161 7 99

N. Triple Crown winner of 1941
130 76 114 152 50 164 80 174 59

O. Play featuring Shylock and Portia (with "P") (2 wds.)
78 141 91 149 177 186 41 169 55 106 98

P. See clue "O" (2 wds.)
107 44 71 128 165 1 156 21

Q. The Ronettes' first hit, in 1963 (3 wds.)
176 35 88 132 14 146 57 163

R. Centaur killed by Hercules
185 94 127 175 36 52 67 196

S. Best Picture of 1984
82 173 89 9 29 101 143

T. Author of *The Executioner's Song* (2 wds.)
2 25 62 17 111 43 54 118 12 70 134 162

U. Delayed results
131 92 105 139 171 73 122 183 148 157 112 23

V. Broadway actress Dorothy
121 33 103 46 190 4

W. Notorious
116 8 184 123 34 195 137 145

X. Italians, Germans, etc.
170 159 65 93 191 187 136 20 28

Y. Bumppo of *The Leatherstocking Tales*
48 153 110 115 56

SOLITAIRE HANGMAN

As in the two-player version of Hangman, the object of this solitaire challenge is to guess the identity of a word before being "hanged."

To begin, choose any letter of the alphabet that you think might be in word I below. Suppose you pick E. Go to the Letter Chart on the facing page and find the number listed in row E of Column I (because you are working on word I). The number is 22; you now look in box number 22 in the Position Chart (to the right of the Letter Chart) and find the number 7. This means the letter E occurs in the seventh position (and nowhere else) in word I. If a letter occurs more than once in a word, the Position Chart will show all its locations.

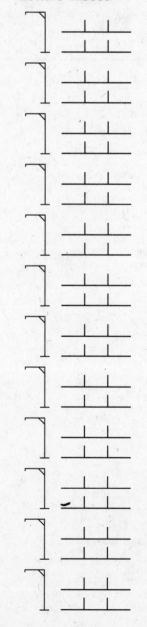

If you find from the Position Chart that a letter appears in position 0, then that letter does not appear in the word. As a penalty for an incorrect guess, you must draw part of a stick figure below the scaffold beside the word blanks. On your first incorrect guess, draw the head; on the second, the body; and on the next four, the arms and legs. If you complete the figure (that is, make six incorrect guesses) before identifying the word, you are "hanged."

If you can identify 8 of the 12 words before being hanged, either you're psychic or you have a remarkable gift for words.

ANSWERS, PAGE 115

Words to Be Guessed

I. $\frac{}{1}$ $\frac{}{2}$ $\frac{}{3}$ $\frac{}{4}$ $\frac{}{5}$ $\frac{}{6}$ $\frac{}{7}$

II. $\frac{}{1}$ $\frac{}{2}$ $\frac{}{3}$ $\frac{}{4}$ $\frac{}{5}$ $\frac{}{6}$ $\frac{}{7}$ $\frac{}{8}$ $\frac{}{9}$

III. $\frac{}{1}$ $\frac{}{2}$ $\frac{}{3}$ $\frac{}{4}$ $\frac{}{5}$ $\frac{}{6}$ $\frac{}{7}$

IV. $\frac{}{1}$ $\frac{}{2}$ $\frac{}{3}$ $\frac{}{4}$ $\frac{}{5}$ $\frac{}{6}$ $\frac{}{7}$ $\frac{}{8}$ $\frac{}{9}$

V. $\frac{}{1}$ $\frac{}{2}$ $\frac{}{3}$ $\frac{}{4}$ $\frac{}{5}$ $\frac{}{6}$ $\frac{}{7}$ $\frac{}{8}$ $\frac{}{9}$

VI. $\frac{}{1}$ $\frac{}{2}$ $\frac{}{3}$ $\frac{}{4}$ $\frac{}{5}$ $\frac{}{6}$ $\frac{}{7}$ $\frac{}{8}$ $\frac{}{9}$

VII. $\frac{}{1}$ $\frac{}{2}$ $\frac{}{3}$ $\frac{}{4}$ $\frac{}{5}$ $\frac{}{6}$ $\frac{}{7}$ $\frac{}{8}$ $\frac{}{9}$

VIII. $\frac{}{1}$ $\frac{}{2}$ $\frac{}{3}$ $\frac{}{4}$ $\frac{}{5}$ $\frac{}{6}$ $\frac{}{7}$

IX. $\frac{}{1}$ $\frac{}{2}$ $\frac{}{3}$ $\frac{}{4}$ $\frac{}{5}$ $\frac{}{6}$ $\frac{}{7}$ $\frac{}{8}$ $\frac{}{9}$

X. $\frac{}{1}$ $\frac{}{2}$ $\frac{}{3}$ $\frac{}{4}$ $\frac{}{5}$ $\frac{}{6}$ $\frac{}{7}$

XI. $\frac{}{1}$ $\frac{}{2}$ $\frac{}{3}$ $\frac{}{4}$ $\frac{}{5}$ $\frac{}{6}$ $\frac{}{7}$ $\frac{}{8}$

XII. $\frac{}{1}$ $\frac{}{2}$ $\frac{}{3}$ $\frac{}{4}$ $\frac{}{5}$ $\frac{}{6}$ $\frac{}{7}$ $\frac{}{8}$

Letters Missed

Letter Chart

	I	II	III	IV	V	VI	VII	VIII	IX	X	XI	XII	
A	46	54	18	71	83	36	8	93	46	61	71	55	A
B	4	40	90	82	34	41	86	54	65	2	80	86	B
C	54	87	46	52	66	9	80	33	12	11	86	41	C
D	31	66	76	86	54	10	90	4	82	22	31	21	D
E	22	26	50	69	44	23	31	85	50	67	9	93	E
F	66	58	23	13	39	93	82	25	34	18	69	76	F
G	93	23	66	22	69	65	88	76	76	39	93	80	G
H	90	31	62	12	53	86	69	95	14	46	45	37	H
I	47	22	79	98	90	46	22	47	48	42	56	34	I
J	99	19	80	46	48	21	93	58	39	54	95	25	J
K	45	69	65	39	93	6	4	87	28	80	58	23	K
L	67	76	54	64	42	18	48	42	71	45	39	54	L
M	95	82	71	15	46	11	35	66	25	13	19	31	M
N	28	39	11	66	50	61	17	55	36	48	78	48	N
O	97	41	82	62	56	40	9	69	32	62	50	82	O
P	61	56	97	19	7	99	11	23	93	82	17	72	P
Q	6	42	48	31	71	90	39	41	61	21	4	90	Q
R	84	71	4	45	31	38	34	71	5	31	54	18	R
S	56	4	17	48	58	54	85	18	80	51	68	56	S
T	9	50	93	89	38	95	76	80	66	15	34	33	T
U	58	64	56	42	64	50	57	40	42	86	23	19	U
V	34	12	25	11	76	97	95	21	69	23	6	64	V
W	41	61	41	76	95	58	42	11	52	90	61	97	W
X	21	99	21	80	13	76	56	9	86	6	64	39	X
Y	39	18	55	63	32	51	32	46	95	64	37	66	Y
Z	80	6	69	90	99	48	71	82	6	93	99	92	Z

I	II	III	IV	V	VI	VII	VIII	IX	X	XI	XII

Position Chart

1	2	3	4	5
9	1,3	2,6	0	3
6	**7**	**8**	**9**	**10**
0	3	5	0	3,9
11	**12**	**13**	**14**	**15**
0	8	0	9	0
16	**17**	**18**	**19**	**20**
8	4	0	3	8
21	**22**	**23**	**24**	**25**
0	7	0	2,5,9	0
26	**27**	**28**	**29**	**30**
4,9	9	4	3	7,8
31	**32**	**33**	**34**	**35**
0	2	4	0	3,9
36	**37**	**38**	**39**	**40**
7	2,8	8	0	2
41	**42**	**43**	**44**	**45**
1	0	9	5,9	5
46	**47**	**48**	**49**	**50**
0	3	0	3	6
51	**52**	**53**	**54**	**55**
4	1	1,4	0	7
56	**57**	**58**	**59**	**60**
0	8	0	7	1
61	**62**	**63**	**64**	**65**
0	2	4	0	5
66	**67**	**68**	**69**	**70**
0	6	1	0	6
71	**72**	**73**	**74**	**75**
0	6	8	4	5,8
76	**77**	**78**	**79**	**80**
0	6	7	3	0
81	**82**	**83**	**84**	**85**
2	0	7	2	6
86	**87**	**88**	**89**	**90**
0	5	1	9	0
91	**92**	**93**	**94**	**95**
5	5	0	1	0
96	**97**	**98**	**99**	**100**
2	0	6	0	9

FOR MEMBERS ONLY

This diagramless is 21 squares wide by 21 squares deep and has left-to-right symmetry. As a hint, the location of the starting square is given on the bottom right corner of page 127.

ANSWER, PAGE 116

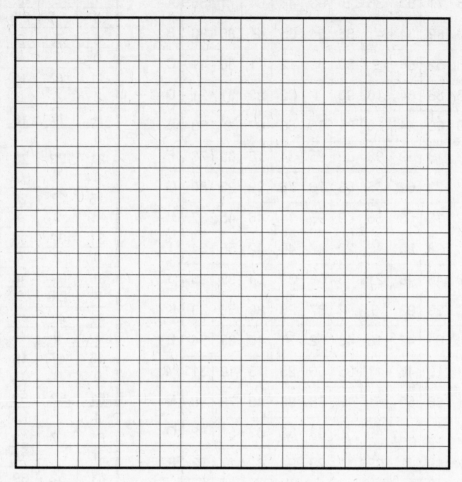

ACROSS

1 Use a ladder
6 Shutdown
8 Athletes' hangout
10 Tramp
11 Evening, in ads
12 Part of TGIF
13 Impresario Hurok
14 Food, informally
16 Invigorates, with "up"
17 Reporters' bosses
19 Witch's concoction
23 "So long," south of the border
24 It was first visited on 7/20/69
28 Tried to lose?
30 Annex
31 Compound leaf stalk
33 Orioles or Blue Jays: 2 wds.
35 *Do the Right Thing* director Spike
36 Like an unshakable alibi
38 Slippery
39 Epsom Downs race
41 Fall to pieces
43 "Whoops!"
44 Humorous in a droll way
45 Oahu souvenir
46 Pronoun type: Abbr.
47 Craggy hill
48 Taste a lollipop
50 Loose language
52 Golf course vehicles
54 Outer: Prefix
55 Singled out
57 Hooter
59 The Literary Guild, for one: 2 wds.
61 Bisect
62 Base-stealer Brock
63 Provoke, as trouble: 2 wds.
64 Nut's partner
65 Watch chain
66 Give the cold shoulder
67 LPs' successors
68 The whole shebang
70 Faucet
73 Pumps up the volume
75 Conductor's baton raisings
76 Camper's set of dinnerware: 2 wds.

DOWN

1 Party mixer: 2 wds.
2 Timber wolf
3 Suffix meaning "somewhat"
4 Subatomic particle
5 Husky fellows
6 Dress
7 Hinders legally
8 The height of fashion
9 Congers
15 Extensively
16 Gathered together
18 Scrabble piece
19 Policeman's stick: 2 wds.
20 Bank (on)
21 Series ending abbr.
22 Fuse
24 Creche figure
25 Autumn mo.
26 River originating at Pittsburgh
27 Cabaret
28 Wisconsin farms
29 Musketeer, at times
31 Theater districts
32 Grow suddenly taller: 2 wds.
33 Plays in the alleys
34 Sandwich need
36 Sour-tasting
37 Beat, as a heart
40 Grain container
42 Pitching stat
49 Relative of lotto
50 Dele-canceling word
51 Putters and pitching wedges: 2 wds.
52 Porterhouse alternative: 2 wds.
53 Drunkards
54 Tan hue
56 XC times V
58 Cherry or pine
60 Family
68 Homecoming guest, for short
69 Canter
71 Voting "nay"
72 Subtle "hey, you!"
74 ___ Moines

BY ROBERT LEIGHTON

Crypto-Funnies 2

Directions appear on page 11.

ANSWER, PAGE 116

1.

2.

3.

4.

BY PETER GORDON

HOOP HOOP HOORAY!

Fill in the 63 basketball-related words and phrases below so they interlock in standard crisscross fashion in the grid. When the puzzle is solved correctly, each word will be used exactly once. A starting hint appears on the bottom left corner of page 127.

ANSWER, PAGE 116

3 LETTERS
ARC
DR. J
FAN
JAM
KEY
NET
PAD
REF
RIM
RUN
SKY
TAP

4 LETTERS
BIRD
DROP
HOOP
LOSS
MISS
N.C.A.A.
PALM
PASS
ROLL
SUNS

5 LETTERS
BLOCK
BULLS
HOYAS
SHOOT
SWISH
TIMER
WEAVE

6 LETTERS
BOARDS
LAKERS
PACERS
PLAYER

POST-UP
REJECT
SIXERS
TRAVEL

7 LETTERS
AIR BALL
ALL-STAR
ASSISTS
CELTICS
PISTONS
REBOUND
SCREENS

8 LETTERS
ALLEY-OOP
BASELINE
JUMP BALL
OFFICIAL
OVERTIME
SLAM DUNK
SNEAKERS
TARHEELS

9 LETTERS
"AIR" JORDAN
BACK COURT

CAVALIERS
FIELD GOAL
PIVOT FOOT
TECHNICAL

11 LETTERS
ABDUL-JABBAR
CHAMBERLAIN

13 LETTERS
DOUBLE DRIBBLE
REVERSE LAY-UPS
THREE-POINTERS

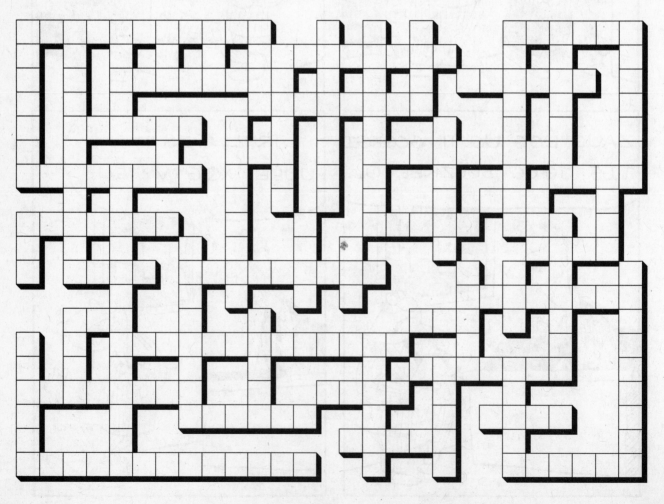

CROSS ANAGRAM

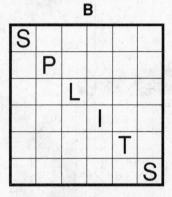

Here's a puzzle for anagram fanciers. With the help of the letters in the grids, answer the clues to discover six pairs of six-letter anagrams. Each answer in grid A has the same letters, rearranged, as the answer on the same line in grid B. (Answers read across only, not down.)

ANSWER, PAGE 116

A

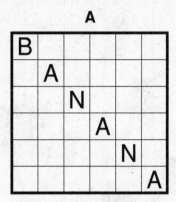

1
2
3
4
5
6

B

CLUES "A"

1 Woman's undergarment, of old
2 Used a file
3 Christmas tree decoration
4 Narrow water passage
5 Mountain climb
6 Belgrade's home

CLUES "B"

1 Rent again
2 Expand
3 Join, as the Army
4 Matisse, for one
5 Makes into law
6 Mad dog's disease

BEYOND THE PALE

Here's a puzzle that should put things in black and white ... well, white, anyway. The answer to each clue below is a word, phrase, or name containing the word WHITE. For example, the clue "Like an executive's job" would lead to the answer WHITE-COLLAR, while "Nickname for New York's theater district" would be GREAT WHITE WAY. How many of these "whites" can you write?

ANSWERS, PAGE 116

1. Walt Disney heroine _____
2. Chicago baseball team _____
3. 1600 Pennsylvania Avenue residence _____
4. *Wheel of Fortune* hostess _____
5. Garage sale item _____
6. When linens are half-price _____
7. Moonshine, commonly _____

8. Quail that's named for its cry _____
9. Bing Crosby holiday song _____
10. Lois Lane's *Daily Planet* boss _____
11. Small fib _____
12. Friend of the Mad Hatter _____
13. 1905 Jack London novel _____
14. Old jazz great _____

BY JANE MADDEN WELCH

Loose Change

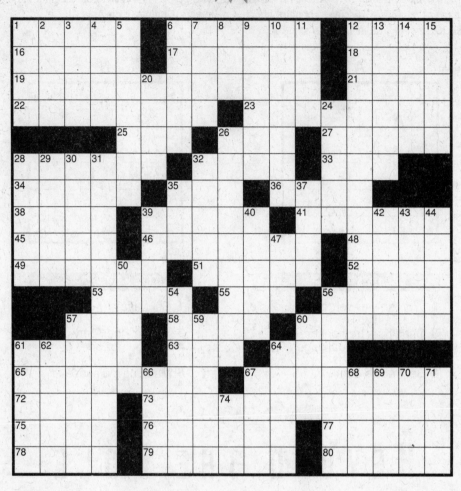

ANSWER, PAGE 117

ACROSS

1 "Three's a ___"
6 Soft wool for sweaters
12 Revolutionary hero Nathan
16 The "A" in A/V
17 Doctor's paging device
18 Greek vowels
19 Comes to a very sudden halt: 4 wds.
21 Departures' opposite: Abbr.
22 Stringer of beads, for example
23 Sudden plunge: 2 wds.
25 Berlin's country: Abbr.
26 Teacher's favorite

27 Bluish green shades
28 Curtains
32 Give up, as territory
33 Juicy Fruit, for example
34 Picture puzzle
35 Enthusiast
36 New York stadium
38 '60s politico ___ Clayton Powell
39 Aging comic George
41 Take to the police station
45 Will-o'-the-___
46 Feeling jealous
48 Rip (up)
49 Villains' "smiles"
51 New York's immigration island
52 Buffalo's lake
53 "Doggone it!"

55 TV's ___ My Children
56 Beverage
57 Roadside tavern
58 ___ Express
60 Fixes the time, as on a clock
61 Become terror-stricken
63 "___ You Lonesome Tonight?"
64 Tipsy sound
65 Mao's nation: 2 wds.
67 Singer
72 Actor Estrada
73 Early jukeboxes
75 King, in formal address
76 Pitcairn or Easter
77 Devour completely: 2 wds.

78 Good Housekeeping ___ of Approval
79 Letters after 18-Across
80 Glitches

DOWN

1 Play ensemble
2 Book after Judges
3 Smell
4 Use a sponge
5 Prescription amounts
6 "Li'l ___"
7 Close at hand
8 High school equivalency exam: Abbr.
9 Stated a belief
10 VCR controllers
11 Greek war god
12 Command center
13 Entrance hall

14 Creepy-crawly insect stage
15 Lisper's problem letters
20 Lyric poems
24 More than willing
26 1967 Beatles hit: 2 wds.
28 Sketches
29 ___ the face (fuming): 2 wds.
30 Degrade
31 Deli bread
32 Whittle
35 "Are we having ___ yet?"
37 Old witches
39 The tops
40 Frivolous
42 Spooky
43 ___ Valentine's Day
44 Long journeys
47 Zilch

50 Cattleman's home
54 Madrid language
56 The Gay Nineties and the Roaring Twenties
57 Indian Prime Minister Gandhi
59 Delphi answerer
60 Puerto ___
61 Use an iron
62 Eagle's home
64 Grasps
66 "What's ___ for me?": 2 wds.
67 ___ cava (major vein)
68 Tilt
69 Little bit
70 ___ as a bug in a rug
71 Recipe amounts: Abbr.
74 "Krazy ___" of cartoons

PENCIL POINTERS 3

In this crossword the clues appear in the grid itself. Enter the answers in the direction of the pointers.

ANSWER, PAGE 117

The grid contains the following clues:

Row / Position	Clue
	Small-pox shot
	Singer Lane
	Actress Holm
	Dirty Harry star
	"___ a Small World"
	Common gaseous element
	Autry or Rayburn
	Cuba's Fidel
	Cop's badge
	From ___ to bottom
	Fills in for
	Popular Nabisco cookie
	Cleo's snake
	Bowler or fedora
	___ *One* (Prez's plane)
	Twisted, as humor
	Dog's warning sound
	Houston baseball player
	Writer Irwin ___ Periods
	Hitting hard
	Job for a cobbler
	Finger swelling
	One who leaves a gratuity
	Attempt
	Light switch settings
	Unusual Salami shops
	Mauna ___
	Sour notes
	Pig's cry
	Rip
	Person twixt 12 & 20
	Didn't sit / Curse
	Crowbars, e.g.
	Gymnast Korbut
	Leave in a hurry
	Deity
	Casey of baseball
	Turn up, as a clue
	What's Up, ___?
	Health resort
	Italian money
	Wormed (out of)
	Title givers
	___ Moines, Iowa
	Indian of Peru / Donkey
	Final
	Song for one
	Suave actor David
	"... a ___ scholar"
	Child punisher
	Wise person
	Attack
	Indian homes
	Inquire
	Using logic
	Bouquet holder
	Other-wise
	Propels a boat
	Three make a yard
	Con-vened again
	Mailed off
	First tennis shot
	"Half ___ is better than ..."
	Parts of a play
	Actor Erwin
	Genuine
	Religious groups
	Figures of speech
	Pert talk
	Larry, Moe, or Curly
	Pro-found
	Sandra and Ruby
	Blowing a horn
	Aroma
	Item used in a play
	Catch sight of
	Roast ___ sandwich
	Before, to poets
	Crafty negoti-ator
	Holiday of Vietnam
	Sly laugh
	Abate / Coal source
	"Roses ___ red"
	Whole numbers
	Bird's home
	Jealous feeling
	Carl Sagan book
	Sugar bowl's mate
	Arrested / Prime periods
	A Great Lake
	Gin and ___
	Girl in a B'way show
	Actor Sean
	Awful smell / Demean
	Atones for
	Kid's coin saver
	1/12 of a foot
	Actress Gardner / Blood
	Frozen water / Freshly
	Bridge of San Luis ___
	Get older
	Obtain
	Young boy
	Timid
	Nabokov novel
	Greek letter
	Charged atom
	"Ready, ___, go!"
	Cambodia's Lon ___
	Opposite of devils
	Noisy birds
	Paper fold
	College cheer
	Ugly sight
	That girl
	Mother sheep
	They color fabrics
	Meet Me ___ Louis

BY NICK NORTH

ABSOLUTELY BATTY

Bats are strange beasts, hanging upside-down all day in the dark, and flapping about, shrieking all night.

Chiropterologists tell us that bats "see" by sonar—but not too well. Frankly, if we were flying around in the middle of the night with no lights, we'd probably do a fair amount of shrieking, too.

Each of the 51 "bat" words and phrases listed below is hidden in the grid. As usual, an answer may read horizontally, vertically, or diagonally, but always in a straight line. As you'll see, each time the letters B-A-T appear in a word, they have been replaced by a bat symbol in the grid. We hope this doesn't drive you bats (groan). *ANSWER, PAGE 117*

(word-search grid with bat symbols replacing the letters B-A-T)

C																	H		
O	M														E	🦇			
S	I	N												T	H	H			
E	O	T	🦇	M			Z	A				H	E	C	G	S			
A	🦇	R	R	T	E		O	C	D		🦇	H	E	T	I	C			
🦇	A	N	E	Y	E	L	E	N	M	R	S	A	H	🦇	B	A	S	U	D	K	F	O
R	R	A	T	E	N	🦇	C	I	M	O	🦇	U	S	H	🦇	E	I	T	O	🦇	U	R	X	🦇
E	Y	M	T	O	V	O	E	B	🦇	M	H	A	L	O	D	R	A	S	C	K	🦇	U	N	M
P	I	R	H	🦇	T	A	L	I	O	N	E	B	G	H	R	E	T	A	M	🦇	A	T	S	O
R	T	O	E	U	🦇	S	C	C	N	H	G	E	G	M	I	🦇	R	E	V	E	N	A	S	B
O	E	N	J	T	F	T	I	🦇	R	L	R	H	R	O	B	W	L	K	🦇	N	O	A	L	I
🦇	🦇	H	O	S	🦇	🦇	H	R	O	B	E	S	A	F	R	B	S	A	B	🦇	I	C	A	L
E	O	I	🦇	A	A	N	T	T	U	H	E	H	🦇	B	A	J	E	M	C	W	🦇	L	T	E
R	N	H	N	D	L	O	L	G	R	K	🦇	T	🦇	H	H	O	U	S	E	O	I	S		
P	C	A		U	H	T	A	E	R	B	D	E	🦇	H	T	I	W	D		R	M	I		
P	U	N		S			A	T	D	N	E				N				P	🦇	🦇			
A	🦇	D					N	X	D	T	K								Y	R	E			
O							S	E	I											E	E			
R							O	🦇	O												E			
							N	A	N															
								N																
								U																

ABATTOIR	BATHETIC		MAKE A STAB AT	SUBATOMIC
ACERBATE	BATHHOUSE		MELBA TOAST	SUNBATHER
ACROBATIC	BATHOS	BATTERY	NORMAN BATES	THE JOB AT HAND
ALBATROSS	BATHROBE	BATTLEAXE	PROBATION	TURKISH BATH
ANABATIC	BATHSHEBA	BIRDBATH	REBATE	UNABATED
APPROBATE	BATIK	CLIMB A TREE	REPROBATE	VERBATIM
BATAAN	BATISTA	COMBAT	RUBATO	WITH BATED
BAT AN EYE	BATMOBILE	DEBATABLE	SABBATH	BREATH
BATCAVE	BATON ROUGE	GRAB ATTENTION	SABBATICAL	WOMBAT
BATEAUX	BATTALION	INCUBATOR	STABAT MATER	ZORBA THE
BATHCHAIR	BATTEN	JABBA THE HUTT	STUB A TOE	GREEK

DOUBLE CROSS 3

Directions appear on page 15.

ANSWER, PAGE 117

1R	2P	3F	4I	5C		6A	7W	8E	9C	10G		11N	12F		13A	14O	15I	16E	17K	18B	19C
20J	21Q	22D		23K	24T	25V	26A	27O	28G		29R	30P	31C	32H	33T		34Q	35W	36D	37L	38O
	39N	40J	41A	42Q	43I	44M	45W		46W	47U	48E	49L	50K	51H		52P		53O	54N	55W	56S
57M	58T	59B	60Q	61D		62C	63U	64F		65N	66A	67I	68W	69B	70C	71D	72S		73J	74N	
75I	76R	77K	78H		79V	80O	81T	82D		83J		84A	85P	86C	87L		88S	89Q	90N		91G
92E	93I		94V	95A	96B	97U		98V	99C	100O	101Q	102H	103L	104D	105K	106R		107T	108B	109Q	126A
110V		111N	112E		113J	114M	115K		116R	117O		118U	119V	120D	121H		122W	123E	124Q	125B	126A
	127T	128R	129W		130L	131I	132F	133P	134D	135W	136N	137H	138V		139E	140T		141I	142O	143S	144N
145Q	146T	147B		148G	149K		150O	151S	152M	153L		154F	155D	156C	157N	158U	159S		160A	161I	162W
163C	164R		165H		166M	167N	168I	169E		170F	171R	172J	173A	174S	175W	176B		177P	178M	179N	180U

A. Mary Frann's former sitcom costar (2 wds.)
13 26 41 173 66 6 84 95 126 160

B. Christ, as the Messiah
176 18 59 69 96 108 125 147

C. 1941 Bette Davis film (2 wds.)
156 19 62 86 31 5 99 9 163 70

D. Pests
104 134 155 22 36 61 120 71 82

E. City for which Wayne Gretzky first played
92 8 112 139 169 16 48 123

F. Start of a basketball game (hyph.)
170 3 154 64 132 12

G. They're bagged at the supermarket
91 10 148 28

H. Storied Apache chief
137 102 32 121 165 51 78

I. Character actor married to Anne Jackson (2 wds.)
93 131 141 75 168 4 15 43 67 161

J. Italian port on the Adriatic
20 40 73 83 113 172

K. Grant money?
23 105 77 115 17 50 149

L. Perfectly (3 wds.)
37 103 130 49 87 153

M. Loser at El Alamein
44 114 152 166 178 57

N. Revolutionary War tune (2 wds.)
74 111 136 157 167 179 65 11 144
90 39 54

O. Jason's crew
80 100 53 117 142 14 27 38 150

P. Combustible used in flamethrowers
30 52 177 85 133 2

Q. Ira Levin Broadway thriller
124 21 60 101 145 109 42 89 34

R. Baa-a-ashful?
106 128 1 29 164 76 116 171

S. #1 Otis Redding tune of 1968 (with "T") (2 wds.)
56 88 159 72 151 143 174

T. See Clue "S" (3 wds.)
146 140 127 33 58 107 24 81

U. Animal-kingdom division
180 63 97 158 47 118

V. Egyptologist's exhibits
25 119 94 98 110 138 79

W. Jim Hutton's detective role (2 wds.)
162 175 68 7 35 45 46 122 129
135 55

JUMBO CROSSWORD 1

ANSWER, PAGE 117

ACROSS

1 Esprit de corps
7 Flicks of the finger
14 Give a face-lift to
20 Get ___ one's head: 2 wds.
21 Vast
22 Having no key
23 Apron spots
24 More like a marsh, perhaps
25 Congress-woman Waters
26 Mortar carrier
27 Emphasize
29 Chaplinesque types
31 60 secs.
32 Detroit product
34 Comedian Kabibble
35 Numbers man, for short
36 NaCl
37 Gardener, in a way
41 Hidden flaw of character: 3 wds.
44 Interoffice notes
45 The Time Machine author
47 Israeli circle dances
48 Ball game statistician
50 U.S. spy org.
51 "Mind over ___"
54 Put into words
56 Kicky Cuban dance

58 Opening to peep through
59 Screenwriter Anita
60 Longtime Boston Celtics coach: 2 wds.
63 Periods of prominence
64 Rainbow's shape
65 Problem with esses
66 ___ breve (2/2 time)
67 Jr.'s son
68 Mexican snack
70 Mind: It.
71 Closes in on
73 Lady's escort
74 None too bright
76 Arboreal play spots
78 The Emerald Isle
79 "Jose Jimenez" comic
80 With the river's current
86 Peter Pan actress: 2 wds.
92 Small bills
93 Language of India
94 Linda Lavin's old sitcom
95 Bond foe: 2 wds.
96 Lb. and oz.
97 Yoko's kin
98 Avatar of Vishnu
99 Musical sensitivity
100 On-___ inspection
102 Very loose approximation
105 Have the gumption

106 Comes out of the woodwork
108 Race: Prefix
109 Deep divisions
111 Pulpit oration
112 Before, poetically
113 All-devouring insect
114 Debonair actor David
116 Sudden gush
118 Rhino's South African cousin
119 Milky feldspars
122 Tourists
126 Pinnacle
127 "Bei ___ Bist Du Schoen"
128 Carol syllable
129 Actress Perlman of Cheers
130 Sault ___ Marie
131 Controls the rudder
134 Rooming units
137 Letters on some American ships
138 Simple cotton cloth
140 Cry of derision
142 Office pool members
144 Like some streets
145 Everlasting
146 Be a snitch
147 Grand ___ (Wyoming range)
148 Bird dogs
149 Humiliated

DOWN

1 Accident
2 Traveling, as a band: 2 wds.
3 1942 Hope/Crosby picture: 3 wds.
4 Bird: Prefix
5 Camera part
6 Formerly, formerly
7 Sherwood, for one
8 Skating entertainment: 2 wds.
9 Bottom of a wine barrel
10 Boy
11 "What's ___ for me?": 2 wds.
12 Prepares ears for earrings
13 Fracas
14 Highway exit
15 H's ancestors
16 ___ populi
17 What Beatrix Potter wrote: 2 wds.
18 Philippines capital
19 More than enough
28 Narrow inlets
30 SAT section
33 Thaïs and Tosca
36 Harshly criticize
38 Actor Ed of Daniel Boone
39 Horn-using bull
40 Earned back, as losses
41 Glaring
42 Sex appeal
43 Brawl

46 Bank-goer's bane
48 Lands like a plump tomato
49 Like some Sunday singing
52 Benjamin's love in The Graduate
53 Convenes again
55 Harmful
56 Indian social division
57 Fitter
58 Cowardly types
61 By ___ of (because of)
62 Wings
69 Olympic track great Jesse
70 Merriment
72 Humble pie
73 Gridiron lineman
75 Ill. neighbor
77 "Not ___ bet!": 2 wds.
80 Uses a divining rod
81 Punctual: 2 wds.
82 Breakfast dish with ham and peppers: 2 wds.
83 Feminine suffix
84 Give ___ of one's own medicine: 2 wds.
85 Errors in judgment
86 Kingdome team
87 San Antonio landmark
88 Ottava ___ (verse stanza)

89 Puzzling party doings: 2 wds.
90 Up ___ (indignant): 2 wds.
91 "There's ___ for the weary": 2 wds.
101 White weasel
102 Author of The Maids
103 By way of, for short
104 Showy display
105 More risky
107 Statehouse VIPs: Abbr.
110 Malt liquor ingredient
115 Alaskan seaport
116 Like a saw's edge
117 In name only
118 One of those things
119 Good-luck figure
120 Car fuel rating
121 Sister's daughters
123 Throws on the barbecue
124 Repair Oxfords
125 Was a smart-mouth
131 Look over
132 Kid's stocking stuffers
133 Dele the "dele"
134 In one's right mind
135 "¿Como ___ usted?"
136 Use a dagger
139 ___ Jima
141 Computer monitor: Abbr.
143 Approx. hour when due in

DSZQUPHSBNT! 1

Below are seven messages—consisting of pithy sayings, fascinating facts, and a cartoon gag—that have been translated into simple cipher alphabets. Letter substitutions remain constant throughout any one cipher, but change from one cipher to the next, and the level of difficulty increases as you progress. An asterisk (*) indicates a proper noun or title. *ANSWERS, PAGE 117*

1. CRYPTOON

YOWT ZEWWT, ZUW...XKUZ
PUMOXUDO HIWWIQXT
JPOIWPT ZXIXOZ UX'Z
EQPT YIPUN MEW XKO
PUMO EM XKO HIXJK.

2. THAT'S IT?

PIYYXPP QE FX BP WTOBDV
QXD WEDXSZXN FXCEDP
TDZ XTQBDV EDCS QWX
QEL WTCA EA XTYW EDX.
—*UTKUKT *PQKXBPTDZ

3. WRONG SIZE

T KOLLUYGN KNLUM WZVW
TV VOL *KOUZWVETW CZYV
LJKOTRCL KSGRVLU,
IZWOZRC LHLUQSRL
ETRQ "OTXXQ ULVGURW."

4. I'LL TOO

DZW QWG KIWJJPQE YWW
AZOFI, KWQD KZVIIPQE YM
ZWS FVF, AOQ'D NPQX
"*NSVVD *JVVIK," "*DM-
*X-YVJ," VS "*SWXXP GPI."

5. NIGHT VISION

FUY TSP OUSIRM LFDORR,
ZVHFISUM, SPY YRPLDERM
FP LSZUR ZRHFER ZRY;
PRSEMVXWLRY CVHR
LWVPGM WVM WRSY WSM
HSUURP FHH.

6. JUSTICE?

GNORO GWOUR GVQYF
GWXT, GNDDRXZAU, "GWFY
GRRX GNTSNQMRXF, GNZQ
GVEAF, GRYYZFVA
GWAMZRF."

7. LOOK AT THE TIME!

VNTJC PNYAO ZHALV
ATIVC LIFHV JNYAH KUTIO
RTAWV FIOQH JHXUC
QIHVL, "XUHF'L LNHVH
QUHXL, *RUXFW?"

JIGSAW BOXES

The object of Jigsaw Boxes is to fit the pieces into the squares to form an interesting message. To begin, note that the grid is divided into 16 sections (A-1, A-2, B-1, etc.) and that the jigsaw pieces are organized at the side by section. Fit the pieces into the appropriate sections of the grid (across only) to form the message reading across line by line. Black squares separate words in the message, and words not stopped at the end of one line will continue on the next. In section A-1 there is only one three-letter piece, so we've filled it in for you. You take it from there.

ANSWER, PAGE 117

A-1
R
IN
~~THE~~
AMED
ORER

A-2
BY
LIV
ZAI
ARUW

A-3
W
RE
IMI
THE
INGS

A-4
N
AS
EXPL
RIVE
TONE

B-1
H
S
IT
ON
RI
TIVE

B-2
E
AS
WHA
DISC
VERS

B-3
T
IS
KED
NAM
OVER

B-4
A
E
NA
TH
ING
THI

C-1
E
N
NA
SA
ARU
WHA

C-2
T
IS
TIVE
WIMI
YING

C-3
LIV
MEA
REP
THI

C-4
S
MA
INGS
LIED
NING

D-1
A
OD
HAS
TONE
UWIM

D-2
I
T
EV
ND
BEE
MIS

D-3
N
R
S
ER
HE
TH
UNDE

D-4
E
AR
INCE
IVER
RSTO

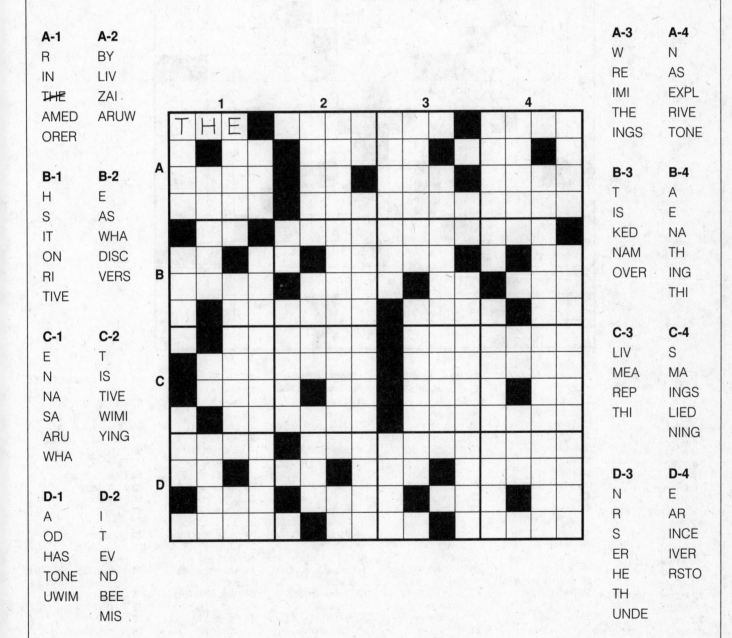

ACROSS

1 1-Across, for example
7 Hurricanes
13 D.C. summer setting
16 Inducement
17 Protects in a gunfight
18 New beginning?
19 Part of an international breakfast?: 2 wds.
21 Large antelope
22 Place to get hitched
23 Free (of)
24 Smudge
25 Exemplar of patience
28 White or Green, in "Clue"
30 Fly without an engine
31 Carpet calculation
33 Penna. city
34 Wiped out
35 Baloney
37 Approves
38 Hasty
39 Youngster's fear
42 Send a signal
46 Connecticut collegian
47 Very long time
48 Baseball great Mel
49 Employ
50 Editor's concern
53 Represented: 2 wds.
55 Astronaut Armstrong
56 Prized possession
58 Throw a fastball
59 Takes a second?
61 Zorba, for instance
64 Jokes around
65 Bradley and Sharif
66 Bee participant
68 Teacher's org.
69 Long sentence?
70 Gerard of *Buck Rogers in the 25th Century*
71 Lucy's brother
73 Prime-time alien
74 Part of an international breakfast?: 2 wds.
79 Zilch
80 Pennsylvania, for one
81 *Glitz* writer Leonard
82 Stag's mate
83 Annoy
84 Apartment dweller

DOWN

1 Mantras
2 Soda
3 Letter between ζ and θ
4 Ship of 1492
5 Lesser of two ___
6 Prepare for a big day: 2 wds.
7 Nemesis in *The Adventures of Captain Marvel*
8 Mr. Thumb
9 Cloudy
10 Ignited again
11 TV talker of yore: 2 wds.
12 Transatlantic speedster
13 Part of an international breakfast?: 2 wds.
14 Strip
15 Saw the sights
20 Corned-beef concoction
24 Designer Bill
25 Made a quick punch
26 Baltimore baseballer
27 Part of an international breakfast?: 2 wds.
29 Lodge animal
30 Scholarship source
32 Bronze or Ice
34 Muse of poetry
36 Blinkers?
40 Drudges
41 Actress Jillian
43 Erode
44 Wagner's *Tristan und* ___
45 Famous Mother of mercy
51 Big name in tractors
52 Purple vegetable
53 More malodorous
54 Hägar creator Browne
57 Before, to Shakespeare
59 Charlemagne's nephew
60 *Young Guns* star Estevez
62 Director Kazan
63 Mutt motel
66 Trig ratios
67 Russian cabbage?
70 Donated
72 Adams and Houston
74 Yankee Doodle wore one
75 Owed
76 TV's Bill, for short
77 Mine find
78 Society page word

DOUBLE FEATURES

We don't like to impose on our readers, but in this case we thought we'd make an exception. Showing below are 15 "double features" where the name of one movie is superimposed over the name of another. Your job is to determine what two movies are showing at each double feature. If you prove true to type, you won't need to check the ...

ANSWERS, PAGE 118

1. BpoadCaypseNNws

2. NaaïonglSaddlet

3. TheeBCrds

4. Shane

5. TheaChoduMae

6. Real Window

7. Casablanca

8. BohaleAandaClyde

9. CatBamba

10. CommingahoGaAmefica

11. RoboMep

12. Dual Metel Mardet

13. AiChyrDanting

14. MaerPedntesshBrMde

15. MIAxSOH

BY NICK NORTH

DÉJÀ VU

These days, television reruns pop up at all times of year, so here's an appropriate crisscross for any season. Enter the name of each old TV series below into the grid in standard crisscross fashion, **except** that, due to repeat episodes, you may fill in an answer more than once. Words in parentheses are not to be entered into the grid. A starting hint appears on the bottom left corner of page 127.

ANSWER, PAGE 118

4 LETTERS
FAME
M*A*S*H
TAXI

5 LETTERS
ALICE
(*The*) A-TEAM
(*The*) BARON
RHODA

6 LETTERS
CHEERS
HARRY-O
MAGNUM (*P.I.*)

7 LETTERS
BONANZA
DAKTARI
DRAGNET
LAUGH-IN
NEWHART

VALERIE
WEBSTER

8 LETTERS
GET SMART
GUNSMOKE
IRONSIDE
(*The*) LOVE BOAT
MISTER ED
(*The*) OUTSIDER

STAR TREK
T.J. HOOKER

9 LETTERS
(*The*) EQUALIZER
NAKED CITY

10 LETTERS
(*The*) BRADY BUNCH
GREEN ACRES
(*The*) LONE RANGER
(*The*) REAL McCOYS

12 LETTERS
BARNEY MILLER
BAT MASTERSON
SLEDGE HAMMER!

13 LETTERS
ONE DAY AT A TIME
ONE IN A MILLION

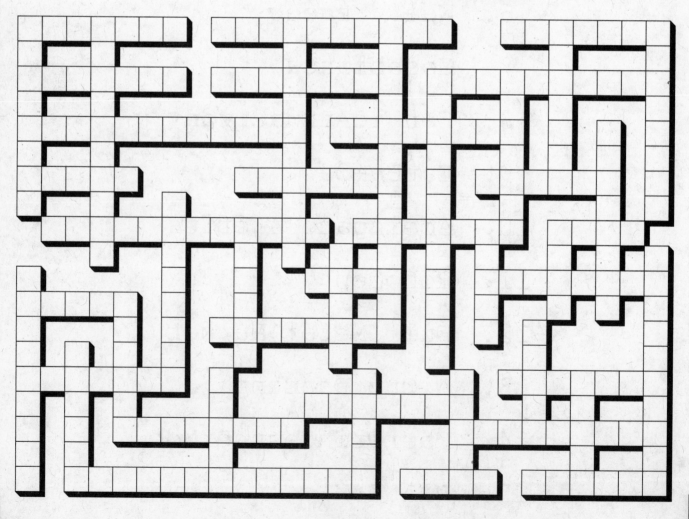

DOUBLE CROSS 4

Directions appear on page 15.

ANSWER, PAGE 118

1J	2H	3E	■	4D	5B	6M	7U	8S	9X	10K	11A	■	12U	13E	14M	15H	16D	17X	■	18M	19B	20Q	21K
22W	23N	■	24C	25P	■	26T	■	27B	28S	29H	30X	31L	32F	33C	34A	35N	36E	■	37V	38B	39I	40P	41T
42R	■	43W	44L	45F	■	46T	47E	■	48S	49G	■	50V	51I	52J	■	53B	54W	55F	■	56P	57H	58K	59M
60D	61V	62N	63C	64R	■	65Q	66H	67B	68E	69W	70L	71P	■	72X	73I	■	74S	■	75M	76O	77N	78E	79V
■	80R	81B	■	82D	83G	84W	85C	86K	87A	■	88H	89B	■	90W	91T	■	92G	93K	94L	■	95D	96E	97S
■	98P	99H	100K	101B	102L	103R	■	104D	105M	■	106G	107A	108Q	109N	■	110C	111I	112D	■	113T	114B	115M	116S
117P	118K	119G	120Q	■	121V	122L	123M	124S	125J	126F	127Q	128P	129N	130E	131B	■	132C	133T	■	134H	135G	136U	137K
138M	139V	■	140B	■	141N	142H	143A	144D	145G	146V	■	147M	148F	■	149L	150C	151P	152O	153K	154W	155E	156X	157H
158S	159B	160T	■	161G	162P	■	163K	164N	165X	■	166K	167D	168B	169V	170G	171R	172O	■	173N	174A	■	175J	176R
■	177G	178W	179M	180L	181E	182B	183C	184O	185K	186R	187T	■	188F	189U	190B	191Q	192D	193J	194L	195R	196M		

A. *Three's Company* star — 87 107 143 174 11 34

B. Arlo Guthrie song based on a Berkshires diner (2 wds.) — 53 19 67 159 81 101 114 131 27 89 140 182 190 38 168 5

C. Chevy model or a famous racehorse — 183 24 63 33 85 110 132 150

D. Author of *Citizen Tom Paine* (2 wds.) — 192 167 104 4 16 60 82 95 112 144

E. Swashbuckler of screen (2 wds.) — 155 181 3 13 68 47 130 36 78 96

F. Dublin's river — 32 126 148 188 45 55

G. Chicory, so-called from the taste of its root — 119 83 92 106 135 145 161 170 49 177

H. Title role for Rosalind Russell (2 wds.) — 15 2 29 66 88 99 57 142 134 157

I. Landlord's due — 39 51 73 111

J. Author of *Uncle Tom's Cabin* — 125 175 1 193 52

K. Steinbeck story of two migrant workers (4 wds.) — 93 153 163 185 166 86 100 118 10 58 137 21

L. What junk food lacks — 44 31 70 94 149 180 194 102 122

M. David Mamet's Broadway hit of 1988 (hyph.) — 179 18 59 105 123 6 196 115 75 138 147 14

N. Capital of Pakistan — 173 23 35 62 141 77 129 164 109

O. Clothing fuzz — 76 152 172 184

P. Countercultural 1969 Dennis Hopper film (2 wds.) — 117 128 25 71 40 56 151 162 98

Q. PBS science series — 108 20 191 65 127 120

R. Movie for which Sophia Loren was named Best Actress (2 wds.) — 195 42 186 80 176 171 64 103

S. Piano company founded in 1853 — 116 8 124 28 158 48 74 97

T. Gilbert and Sullivan's *H.M.S. ___* — 113 46 187 26 91 41 133 160

U. Haymarket Square event, 1886 — 136 7 189 12

V. Plant activity? — 61 37 169 121 50 79 146 139

W. Informs (of) — 54 43 22 69 154 90 178 84

X. Yankees pitcher known as "Gator" — 30 9 72 17 156 165

VINTAGE HUMOR

We may have had a bit too much of the grape ourselves when we came up with this word search. To solve, first find within the grid the 50 types of wine listed below. As always, answers may read horizontally, vertically, or diagonally, but only in a straight line. Some answers, however, will pass over the shaded circles in the grid; in these cases, the letter needed to complete the word should be entered in the appropriate circle. When you're finished, the letters in the circles will spell, from left to right, the conclusion of the sentence above the grid.

ANSWER, PAGE 118

The price of a good wine is ...

```
W L A M B R U S C O C H B E N C N A L B N I N E H C C M E N
D R I N A K T H E M H L N O N I L O N G I R G X T A H E C Y
A R E R I D C H B O A Y F R A S C A T I A N R U T M D S H U
C C H E I S E A S N B S D N F N U L A N S I D A W O I N A L
A J C W ●●●●●●●● S N O L O R A ●●●●●●●● U I R T
S O L A I S N D R R I L N D U N A L R S E B E D V T A H D R
A H I P A P E A Y A S V A N D G G H L E A L P R A I S M O E
E A M C L N T H I C E A I R F R R I I I T E N O O L T E N N
S N U D O B I S Q H U N I C K M N U V L M E Y B S L I U N I
S N A I J S E ●●● C E B R C G U I ●●●●● A L A S R A M
I I R N U A G R R T M R E O A O B S E A A K S A E D P S Y A
U S F R A U O F N E U C H A T E L W C I K S N E L O U A S R
F B B O E T T H A K B O T I N E M D Y A O A T Y E C M U W T
Y E E E B E D T C M A M M G Y M I I D R T N D E D A A L N Z
L R I D S R Y O A Y S S A R O M E V T U R E H L N I N T N R
L G L G ●●●● A C L E P ●●● V O V R O ●●●●● T E R U
I E F M R E O M M T M H E E C V A N C O I K H E F E E N T W
U R M C M S O M E A D Y P L L A Y T H E K N I S N G H B T E
O O S B Y A R I H S G T O P H E A P I N O T N O I R N E A G
P I T S I R H C A M Y R H C A L R S E D I T H M Z R U D Y C
```

AMONTILLADO	CATAWBA	FRASCATI	MEDOC	RETSINA
ASTI SPUMANTE	CHABLIS	GAMAY	MEURSAULT	RIESLING
BAROLO	CHAMBERTIN	GEWURZTRAMINER	MONTRACHET	SAUTERNES
BARSAC	CHAMPAGNE	GRIGNOLINO	MOSELLE	SEMILLON
BEAUJOLAIS	CHARDONNAY	JOHANNISBERGER	MUSCATEL	SHERRY
BERNKASTELER	CHENIN BLANC	LACHRYMA CHRISTI	NEUCHATEL	SOAVE
BLANC DE NOIRS	CHIANTI	LAMBRUSCO	ORVIETO	SYLVANER
BORDEAUX	CLARET	LIEBFRAUMILCH	PINOT NOIR	TOKAY
BURGUNDY	COLD DUCK	MADEIRA	POMMARD	VERMOUTH
CABERNET SAUVIGNON	CORVO	MARSALA	POUILLY-FUISSE	ZINFANDEL

PENCIL POINTERS 4

In this crossword the clues appear in the grid itself. Enter the answers in the direction of the pointers.

ANSWER, PAGE 119

The grid contains the following clues (reading across each row):

- Suffers for past acts
- Sacrifice sites
- "Hello, over there!"
- Lettered game piece
- End of a sock
- Lure
- Lima's land
- Protest, of a sort
- Mass __ (buses & trains)
- Colored kerchief
- Onion-like veggie
- Donkey
- Mob revolt
- Spy __ Hari
- Kilt wearer
- Fire warning sounds
- Crazy
- Bumped into
- Got to one's feet
- He's lost his memory
- Ripped apart
- Con's home
- Explorer Hernando
- "Caught you!"
- Job for a movie daredevil
- Saturate
- Tit for __
- After-bath attire
- First President
- Our Miss Brooks star
- Standard scores
- Wedding cake layer
- Auto lot purchase
- Donny and Marie
- Actor Carney
- Immature insect form
- Homer classic
- Reagan VIP Edwin
- Defeats
- Cry
- Took a risk
- Words of understanding
- Dummy Mortimer __
- Swiss math pioneer
- Steers clear of
- Coffee cake brand
- Withered and dry
- Rising motion
- __ Camera (play)
- Attempts
- Cashew or pecan
- Short-wave
- Blotted
- Golfing pegs
- Very wide, as an ocean
- Magical remedies
- Meager
- Citrus drinks
- Loan out again
- Pigpen
- City of New Jersey
- Primp
- Tennis's Lendl et al.
- Not at all wordy
- Useful quality
- Drags the river bottom
- Clear the slate
- Pouched bread
- Lure
- Roger Daltrey's group
- 50%
- "... lived happily __ after"
- Places for claret bottles
- Blasting stuff
- Rapidly
- "Rocket Man" singer
- Cow's sound
- Karenina
- Starts a tennis game
- Very agreeable aide
- Draws close to
- Relating to birds
- Elk's horns
- Zodiac roarer
- Cast members
- Past or past perfect
- Camera part
- Western Pennsylvania city
- Mini-map
- Pebbles's pet
- Worry
- Light-filling gas
- Fit for either current
- Belgian treaty city
- Surrounding glows
- __-Goldwyn-Mayer
- West German steel city
- One of the Three Bears
- Keep __ (stick in there)
- __ one's laurels
- Type size
- Opera solo
- Rave like a madman
- Draw, in sports
- Joy
- __ and caboodle
- Grant's foe
- Technical lingo
- Tints
- Scouts' org.
- Taunt with a feather
- Midwest TV preacher
- More repulsive
- Actor/dancer Gregory
- Trap
- Samples the soup
- Cager Archibald
- Holmes's doctor friend

HEAD HUNTING

Back before the crossword puzzle (invented in 1913), newspapers sometimes ran daily hidden picture puzzles in which the object was to find a concealed image. One important series of these puzzles was drawn by an artist named Tanner, about whom we know nothing other than that he must have been very busy producing these ingenious illustrations! Each picture has a hidden head. How many of the heads can you find?

ANSWERS, PAGE 119

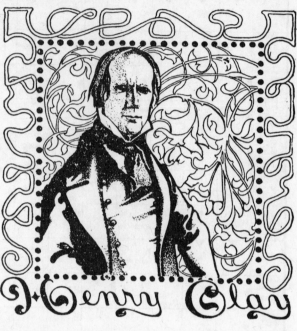

1. Robert Browning, the English poet, and husband of Elizabeth Barrett Browning, is perhaps best known for his long narrative poem *The Ring and the Book*. Find the poet.

2. Henry Clay's skill as an orator and mediator earned him great acclaim and assured him of his position as Speaker of the House of Representatives. Find another Congressman.

3. In 63 A.D., according to Christian legend, the apostle Paul was shipwrecked in Melita. Find another sailor in the storm.

4. On November 16, 1899, American troops in Luzon captured the wardrobe of the wife of Aguinaldo, the Philippine commander. Find his wife.

5. The British Stamp Act of 1765 was to raise revenue in the American colonies for the British Government. It was repudiated by judges, though, and hastily repealed amid intense opposition. Find another judge.

6. Lajos Kossuth, the Hungarian patriot and statesman, led an uprising in 1848 that established a short-lived Hungarian independence. Find another revolutionary.

7. On November 13, 1775, the American forces under Richard Montgomery captured Montreal from the British. Find another soldier.

8. The U.S. Cavalry in the late 19th century, though often portrayed as "saving the day," was itself vulnerable to ambushes by hostile Indians. Find a hidden Indian.

So Long

ANSWER, PAGE 119

ACROSS

1 Partonesque
6 Tractor trailers
11 Proposal
16 "With this ring ___ wed": 2 wds.
17 Make one
18 Moth attractor
19 Affidavit certificate, in law
20 Milk buys
21 Trendy mattress
22 Metal sources
23 "And away ___!": 2 wds.
24 Dulcinea's adorer
26 They're the pits
28 Product's bar code: Abbr.
29 A mere handful
30 Killer whale movie
31 Priestly headdress
33 Marcos, the shoe lady
36 Passbook data
39 Breathing
40 Heavy and hard to move
42 Ken, for one
44 6-Down's other half
47 The end ___ era: 2 wds.
48 Out of ___
49 Chipped in
50 "… watching all ___ go by": 2 wds.
52 Comedy club sounds
54 Holdup
55 Receptacles
56 Wee, to a Scotsman
59 Singer Daltrey, for short
60 Antiwar demonstrators
65 Libya's "mad dog"
67 Teen's woe
68 Track shape
69 It can start you moving
70 Veranda
72 Barely wound
73 ___ and dangerous
74 Newspaper stories
75 "It's ___" ("No sweat"): 2 wds.
76 ___-one odds
77 Bewitching place?
78 Intended

DOWN

1 Jewel, from the French
2 Automotive about-face
3 One way to get rid of documents
4 Poke fun at
5 Nevertheless
6 Half of a magical word
7 Puzzle
8 Cretan king
9 Addams Family cousin
10 Use of words such as 6-Down/44-Across
11 Where execs work
12 Change
13 Live off the ___ the land: 2 wds.
14 Chew the scenery
15 Sign up for more issues
23 Beaver's dad
25 ___ good (mischievous): 3 wds.
27 Ritzy watch brand
31 Army doc
32 Equestrian activity
33 "___ my lamp beside…": 2 wds.
34 Old Testament book
35 Squared
36 Some surrealist paintings
37 Comb piece
38 Pivots
39 From ___ Z: 2 wds.
41 Too prompt
43 The "acid" of "acid rock"
45 "To fetch a ___ water": 2 wds.
46 Determinant
51 He opened Al Capone's vault
53 Suffix for disturb or allow
55 Turned into
56 Crouch
57 Olympic skier Phil
58 Rhett's last words: 2 wds.
60 Meet the Press bunch
61 Scandinavian
62 Former Mrs. Donald Trump
63 Elia or Lainie
64 Sacked out
66 Song for a couple
71 ___ glance: 2 wds.
72 School of whales

THE SPIRAL

This puzzle turns in two directions. The spiral's Inward clues yield a sequence of words to be entered counterclockwise in the spaces from 1 to 100. The Outward clues yield a different set of words to be entered clockwise from 100 back to 1. Fill in the answers, one letter per space, according to the numbers beside the clues. Keep track of which way you're going and have many happy returns.

ANSWER, PAGE 120

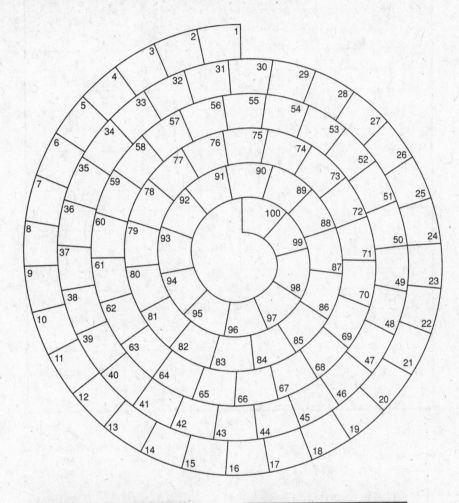

INWARD

1-5	Razor sharpener
6-15	Tells incorrect news
16-22	Falls for a newlywed?
23-29	Kid's "secret" ring
30-36	Freight train segment
37-42	Animal with a busy nose
43-48	___-down (inverted)
49-52	Former Secretary of State Dean
53-59	Crack, e.g.
60-67	Driver with mag wheels
68-73	Some chemical derivatives
74-81	Golden horse
82-87	Rue
88-91	Ditto (with "the")
92-100	1989 movie Steel ___

OUTWARD

100-95	1979 Commodores hit (2 wds.)
94-85	"Dungeons and Dragons" organizer, e.g.
84-77	Skydiver's cry
76-71	Wasn't renewed, as a subscription
70-64	Turkish inns
63-56	Large, fragrant, white flower
55-48	Confident, maybe too much so
47-40	Argumentative one
39-33	Bend, as light
32-26	Fettucine ___
25-21	___ Falls, Iowa
20-14	Con
13-8	Rodeo performers
7-1	Hyundais, Volvos, etc.

DIRTY WORDS

This diagramless is 21 squares wide by 21 squares deep and has left-to-right symmetry. As a hint, the location of the starting square is given on the bottom right corner of page 127.

ANSWER, PAGE 120

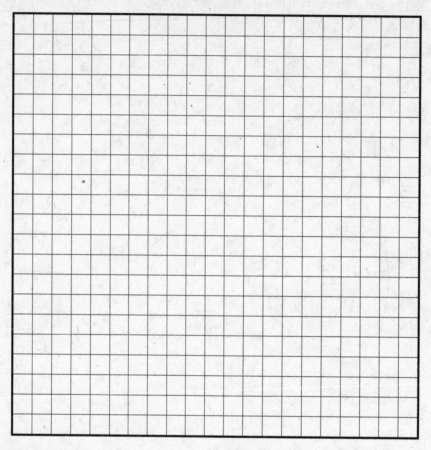

ACROSS

1 Patriotic monogram
4 Tire in the trunk
6 Baby ___ (fortysomething people)
8 Vitamin additive
9 Drinks slowly
11 Make booties
12 Near-eternities
14 Greg Louganis specialty
15 Bar bill
18 Oz visitor
20 Island dance
21 Places for valuables
23 Had on
25 Is blunt: 5 wds.
29 One room in "Clue"
30 Cross, geometrically
31 LXXXIII times V
33 Dodecahedron sides, e.g.
35 Sneakers features
38 Produce eggs
39 Columnist Barrett
40 Quayle's home state: Abbr.
43 Seaside soarer
44 ___ mode: 2 wds.
45 Time-wasting bother
46 Uno doubled
47 Villain's smile
49 Marcus Welby et al.: Abbr.
50 Before, in Berlin
51 Alphabetical man's nickname
52 Skirmishes
54 Attach
55 Slight amount
56 Calculus or trig
57 Sell hotdogs
59 Prefix with angle or athlete
60 Depart
62 Jetsons maid
63 Yale, Brown, Dartmouth, et al., for short
65 Short-lived nuclear particle
66 FDA duty
68 Irritating
70 High-tech Valley
71 Bad toupee
73 Nautical route: 2 wds.
74 Egg boiler's aid
75 Kimono part
76 Lunar valleys
77 Divided by
78 Benefits
80 Platoon setting
81 Egg-shaped
82 Have a congenial relationship (with): 2 wds.

DOWN

1 Second word in fairy tales
2 Sleuth Spade
3 Zeus's warring son
4 Chimney gunk
5 Buffalo's lake
6 Soft white cheese
7 Pip
8 Some hostile attacks
10 Blizzard
11 Do in
13 Plug (up)
14 Stupid dolt
15 VCR need
16 Distantly
17 Flower plots
19 Sources of wise answers
20 Cease
21 Speedy planes
22 Visualizes
24 Icelandic epic
25 "Understand?" in slang: 4 wds.
26 Actress Magnani
27 Aspirin target
28 Archeological activities
29 They're levied identically for all people: 2 wds.
32 Cycling arena
33 ___ of Paris
34 Sticky stuff
36 Finale
37 Tightly packed fish
40 Hip: 3 wds.
41 Aerialist's precaution
42 Researching: 2 wds.
47 Fancy sheet fabric
48 Superman star
52 Wash site
53 Fits of pique
56 Engine
58 Hinder
61 Dutch bloom
62 Car for A.J. Foyt
64 Murdered
65 Biblical song
67 Key ___ pie
69 Songstress Fitzgerald
72 German sub
78 Wetlands area
79 Rep.'s Congressional counterpart

Directions appear on page 11.

ANSWER, PAGE 118

1.

2.

3.

4.

SIGNS OF TROUBLE

To help tourists find their way around town during the upcoming Ragweed Festival, the Ragville Chamber of Commerce has bought 15 new signs, to be erected at various intersections around town (in the positions indicated by dots on the map below). Each will be placed so that drivers approaching an intersection will see the sign on their right. The holes have all been dug, but no one can remember which sign goes where. Can you save the Ragweed Festival by placing each sign in its correct position?

ANSWER, PAGE 119

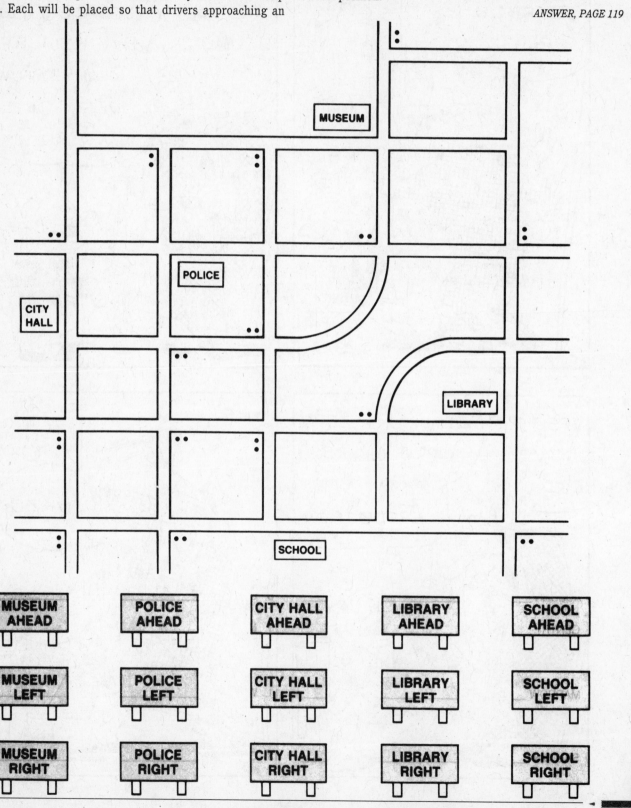

DOUBLE CROSS 5

Directions appear on page 15.

ANSWER, PAGE 119

1V	2B	3A	4N	5O	6G	7D		8Q	9V	10R	11I	12W	13H	14F	15J	16U	17E		18Q	19B	20E	21N	22D	23V
24P	25O		26W	27K	28G		29V	30E	31P	32J		33W	34C	35Y	36T	37K	38I		39B	40G	41W	42M	43Q	44H
45F	46V	47X	48J	49E	50C		51Q	52H		53O	54M	55Y		56F	57I	58M	59Q		60Y	61V	62U	63J	64P	65R
66K	67B		68H	69M	70Q	71D	72V		73G	74T		75J	76F	77P	78I	79W	80M	81U	82D		83K	84V	85L	
86S	87F	88I	89C	90B	91M	92E	93V	94H	95X	96K		97G	98T	99V	100J		101W	102P		103C	104W	105Q		106E
107D	108F		109B	110U	111J	112H		113L	114P	115N	116Y	117D	118A	119W	120J	121E	122G		123S	124H	125Q	126C	127M	128B
129T		130W	131Y	132R		133E	134G	135H	136W		137P	138B	139U	140J		141M	142S	143G		144O	145D	146H	147Q	
148Y	149N	150J	151M	152V		153W	154D	155Y	156H	157E	158P		159U	160M	161W	162G	163X		164N	165Q	166I	167D	168J	169A
	170L		171O	172E	173X	174R	175U	176V	177S	178Q	179J	180B		181Y	182T	183W	184E	185V	186A	187I	188L		189J	190V
191R	192N	193Q	194A		195V	196D		197S	198I	199Y	200H	201W		202V	203G	204P	205B	206L						

A. Piano class?
—3— —118— —186— —169— —194—

B. "Take Me Home Tonight" singer (2 wds.)
—205— —39— —67— —90— —128— —109— —138— —2— —19— —180—

C. Award won by Word "Q"
—34— —50— —89— —103— —126—

D. Bill Cosby book
—196— —167— —154— —7— —22— —71— —107— —117— —145— —82—

E. 1987 Whoopi Goldberg/Sam Elliott film (2 wds.)
—20— —92— —106— —121— —157— —133— —172— —30— —184—
—49— —17—

F. Descend a cliff by means of ropes
—76— —87— —45— —56— —108— —14—

G. 1986 Peace Nobelist, author of *A Jew Today* (2 wds.)
—134— —122— —203— —28— —97— —73— —143— —6— —40— —162—

H. 1959 song by the Falcons (3 wds.)
—68— —124— —13— —146— —156— —200— —44— —52— —94—
—112— —135—

I. Flag position for mourning (hyph.)
—198— —11— —38— —78— —166— —57— —88— —187—

J. *The Jungle* author (2 wds.)
—63— —75— —140— —150— —32— —100— —111— —48— —120—
—179— —15— —168— —189—

K. The Gold Coast, today
—96— —27— —37— —66— —83—

L. Lucifer's domain
—113— —170— —85— —188— —206—

M. Ornamental shield
—42— —58— —127— —80— —141— —151— —54— —69— —160— —91—

N. Amble idly
—115— —149— —164— —192— —4— —21—

O. Where a watch is worn
—144— —171— —5— —25— —53—

P. Not to be entered, by rule (hyph.)
—77— —102— —158— —137— —31— —204— —114— —24— —64—

Q. *Tender Mercies* star (2 wds.)
—193— —51— —178— —165— —18— —59— —147— —125— —8—
—70— —105— —43—

R. Capital of Bangladesh
—132— —174— —191— —10— —65—

S. Elevator passageway
—123— —142— —177— —86— —197—

T. Original Peruvians
—36— —74— —182— —98— —129—

U. Strait
—81— —110— —175— —16— —62— —159— —139—

V. 1987 Stephen King novel (2 wds.)
—202— —61— —190— —93— —9— —29— —46— —99— —152—
—84— —195— —23— —176— —1— —185— —72—

W. 1986 #1 song by Genesis (2 wds.)
—101— —136— —41— —153— —33— —119— —12— —104— —201—
—26— —79— —161— —183— —130—

X. Repair, as with tape
—173— —47— —95— —163—

Y. Maine to Florida (2 wds.)
—55— —181— —148— —60— —35— —199— —131— —155— —116—

PENCIL Y'S

ANSWER, PAGE 120

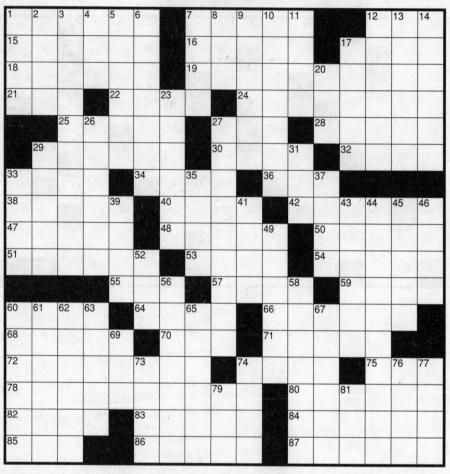

ACROSS

1 Contemporary classical cellist: 2 wds.
7 Relating to an unborn baby
12 Tool with teeth
15 "Yes, Captain": 2 wds.
16 City of central Florida
17 Pocket bread
18 Ventriloquist Willie Tyler's "pal"
19 "Delicious!": 2 wds.
21 Suffix for superlatives and old verbs
22 Baseball's Eddie ("The Walking Man")
24 Stance
25 Spew out
27 Japanese money
28 Beating felt in the wrist
29 Man Friday's friend
30 Whirlpool
32 Gerbils and guppies
33 Actress Dunaway
34 Mobster ___ Diamond
36 It runs in the spring
38 "You ___ Beautiful": 2 wds.
40 Comedienne Martha
42 Assail, like a predator: 2 wds.
47 Bed boards
48 Microscopic opening
50 Speechify
51 Upper bodies
53 Japanese wrestling
54 Room design
55 Droop
57 Painter Chagall
59 Timetable, for short
60 Cummerbund or obi
64 Luke Skywalker's guru
66 Likes and dislikes
68 Neighborhoods
70 Item in Santa's sack
71 Computer entry
72 Gets mud on the rug: 2 wds.
74 School sports org.
75 "Uh-huh"
78 New ___ (Maris or Mantle): 2 wds.
80 Treat worshipfully: 2 wds.
82 Deli breads
83 Stairs
84 Will topic
85 Turf
86 Beans that provide a Chinese sauce
87 One on a quest

DOWN

1 Harvard rival
2 Courtroom cry: Var.
3 Time gone by
4 Bran source
5 "___ Adored You": 2 wds.
6 Spray can type
7 A. J. of Indy 500 fame
8 Old French coin
9 Pressed down firmly
10 Praline nuts
11 Potato-chip brand
12 "Quick as a wink," e.g.
13 Maximally: 2 wds.
14 Newton and Gretzky
17 Accommodate, palindromically: 2 wds.
20 Puppy's bark
23 Navigates
26 Invitees
27 Teacher's response to "Can I leave the room?": 3 wds.
29 Monte ___
31 Big mouth
33 Rapid
35 Gangster's guns
37 Urge
39 Bears: Sp.
41 *Kate and Allie* daughter
43 Mocedades hit song of 1974: 2 wds.
44 Gab
45 Oklahoma Indians
46 Dweeb
49 Of the main artery
52 Utter
56 Entered: 2 wds.
58 Hors d'oeuvres
60 Lascivious men
61 Western gulch
62 Burned somewhat
63 Chops crudely
65 Democrats' mascot
67 Few and far between
69 The limit, sometimes
73 Backtalk
74 *The Untouchables* hero
76 Ending for major or usher
77 Gardener, at times
79 Gas-mileage rating group: Abbr.
81 Had a nosh

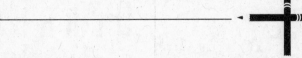

If you have a *way* with words you'll want to get to this puzzle right *away*. Each sentence below can be completed by filling in two words. The second missing word is the same as the first one but with the letter "a" added to the front. For example: A *cute* physician treated the patient's *acute* condition. If you have a *head* on your shoulders you should have no trouble finishing *ahead* of the pack.

ANSWERS, PAGE 118

1. You can't claim to have a _BROAD_ education if you haven't traveled _ABROAD_

2. The puzzle editor wanted to publish a _MAZE_ that would _AMAZE_ his readers, so he designed one that even he couldn't find his way through!

3. Colette liked her talent representative because he was such a _____, a quality not often found in an _____.

4. A _TONE_ in her voice made it clear that she was not about to _ATONE_ for having thrown out her husband's khaki underwear.

5. While waiting for a _MUSE_ to strike so I can write poetry, I sometimes _AMUSE_ myself by solving crosswords.

6. Rats! A _GAIN_ on the scale like this means I'll never be able to eat chocolate mousse _AGAIN_

7. If ever there was a _MOUNT_ destined to _AMOUNT_ to something, it had to be Secretariat.

8. The aging bowler won a _____ even though his skills had begun to _____.

9. As soon as the boxer saw his opponent, he knew that a _____ with him could result in _____ 20 stitches.

10. The cellar needed light, so Chris used a _____ of preserves to hold the door _____.

11. After the dogs picked up a _____ from the bank robber, the posse began its _____ to his mountain hideout.

12. Many novelists would sooner jump off a _____ than have some hack _____ their work for *Reader's Digest*.

13. Sammy Davis Jr. sang only a _____ of "The Star-Spangled Banner," being _____ to straining his vocal cords too much.

14. If you don't send a _____ check to your landlord by the end of the month, you _____ going to have a place to live.

BY ROBERT LEIGHTON

SCRAMBLED COMICS

Some people like their comics over easy, but we prefer ours scrambled. The three comic strips on these pages have had their panels rearranged, with the unfortunate side effect of leaving their punch lines punchless. Can you put them sunny side up? There may be more than one way to arrange a set in a logical sequence, but—*prepare yourself*—only one solution leads to the yolk.

ANSWERS, PAGE 119

TAKE YOUR PICK

A

B

C

D

WHEN SIDNEY MET SHIRLEY

A

B

C

D

BOYS WILL BE BOYS

A

B

C

D

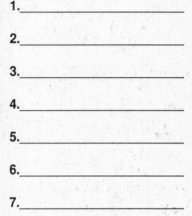

1. _____
2. _____
3. _____
4. _____
5. _____
6. _____
7. _____

1. _____
2. _____
3. _____
4. _____
5. _____
6. _____
7. _____

1. _____
2. _____
3. _____
4. _____
5. _____
6. _____
7. _____

Both words in each paired phrase below are hidden in the grid in typical word search fashion: back & forth, up & down, or diagonally. To make them a bit easier to find, the words in each pair are joined by the crossing of a single letter. For example, SNAKES & SNAILS share an S, as shown below. Are you willing & able to seek & find the others? *ANSWER, PAGE 120*

```
S L L O R J U R Y D O N T S L I A N S
B K B O U E E L D I T F O R K F I R E
O T C D L M C P U N C H E T N H C A K
Y K G O H A H U J E C O N O I I E R A
S E O H S E H C A E P E V I F S B R N
L N J K U R P O T S T C N E E C I O S
R S T I A C O G P O L I S H R N T W W
I P Y D A E R I S D C P I E C E S T H
G I E Y G S T O P A N S D H T S I W T
N H A G I O V S U B U N E N E S V E U
U C S N N L E T Y G U N S X A T S P O
T R L I V E Y E A P H T A E D R R O H
S U C F F A K R E H M T T Y A A R H S
T R R F S R E A F R T I U E Y I T O L
L F A U U N C W E N I H S S R G H U W
O R E T H E N O W N C S I S T H I C K
B T N S S T R I P E S I E S O T N N S
```

BITS & PIECES	GIN & TONIC	NOW & THEN	ROUGH & READY	STRAIGHT &
BOW & ARROW	GUNS & BUTTER	NUTS & BOLTS	SCOTCH & SODA	NARROW
BOYS & GIRLS	HIS & HERS	OVER & UNDER	SHOES & SOCKS	SUGAR & SPICE
CUP & SAUCER	HIT & MISS	PEACHES &	~~SNAKES &~~	THICK & THIN
DEATH & TAXES	HOPE & PRAY	CREAM	~~SNAILS~~	THIS & THAT
EYES & EARS	JUDGE & JURY	POTS & PANS	SPIT & POLISH	TURKEY &
FIRE & ICE	KNIFE & FORK	PUNCH & JUDY	STARS & STRIPES	STUFFING
FISH & CHIPS	LIVE & LEARN	RISE & SHINE	STEAK & EGGS	TWIST & SHOUT
FIVE & TEN	NEAR & FAR	ROCK & ROLL	STOP & GO	WAR & PEACE

SPLIT DECISIONS

The only clues in this crossword are the letter pairs provided in the grid. Each answer across and down consists of two words, which share the letters to be entered in the empty squares. In the example below, the empty squares are filled with the letters O-R-Y to make GLORY and IVORY. Note: a few of the combinations in the grid may have more than one possible answer, but only one will fit with the crossing(s).

ANSWER, PAGE 120

Ex.

CRYPTOLISTS

Below are four lists of related words and phrases that have been translated into simple cipher alphabets. The letter substitutions remain constant within any one group of words (for instance, if V represents G in one word, it will represent G in all the words in that list), but change from one list to the next. A tip to new solvers: Start by thinking of answers that might fit one of the categories, then see if any enciphered words in the list have the same letter pattern.

The fourth list has been left untitled. Solve the code to determine what the items have in common. *ANSWERS, PAGE 121*

1. CHILDREN OF LITERATURE

Ex: Tom Sawyer

L R U R B L P F

W J B Z N U V L J R B B V K Z F

R Q V Z N R

U Z F A U Z T

L Z L L Z Q V F E N U V W C Z F E

V Q Z H R B U G Z N U

J D W C Q R K R B B A Y Z F F

J R Z I Z

Q Z U U Q R Q V B I Y P D F U Q R B V A

L Z F V W W J Z V

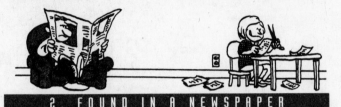

2. FOUND IN A NEWSPAPER

Ex: Advice column

Z T K L X Z Z R G X Q K C

S K W Q R J Q Z X Q C I Z

"E R J T M Y C X R F"

J R X X R L Z X K X E R R F Q X K L

G K S Q G Z

L R Z X Y A L Y C X L R W Q R M Z

E R Y F J Q C R Z

M R Y X E R L L R T K L X Z

Z X K G D T L Q G R Z

E K L K Z G K T R

3. FOOD INSEPARABLES

Ex: Bagels & lox

I L Y B Q A V V G & P A Y V T Y E E I

L A Y H K V T K V V A W & D A E E X

P G E F & Z S S F G A I

U G I Q & Z Q G L I

T Y Z S H & A B B I

Q Y P & Z Q A A I A

U W Y H F I & T A Y H I

T W A Y C & T K V V A W

E A V V K Z A & V S P Y V S

P A Y V & L S V Y V S A I

4. MYSTERY LIST

What do they all have in common?

L G L D A N W W L W

F I M A J C D D N H L

M J C Y I M

M I I Y L C Q I Z W L

N Z K I H I F J A L

D E N Y Z N K J I C R Q I K I

F L Y

H I K J I C R J U K Z E L S J A H

U I H J U W K E J R

F J U G U A L

PENCIL POINTERS 5

In this crossword the clues appear in the grid itself. Enter the answers in the direction of the pointers.

ANSWER, PAGE 121

Left un-harmed	▼	___ Gay (WW2 plane)	Orson Welles role	Stun	Shuttle launch group	Reddish yellow	▼	Pirate's spoils	"That hurts!"	Invite	Lock's partner	Ming *objet d'art*	▼	U.S.A. neigh-bor	Horse-back riding	Cows chew them	Cad	Other-wise
Pie-making nut					___ and dagger	▼						*Cocoon* actor Don						
1978 Belushi movie												Follow-up story						
Rosters						Boxer Balboa Bundle						Radiates						
Henry VIII's daughter									West Virginia capital		North Carolina capital	Pacino and Capone	Cast a ballot	Man or Capri				
Stupor					Teen problem	No ifs, ___, or buts	Dele undoer		Necktie							Beatles' "Eleanor ___"	Arrives	Trap
Famous NYC terminal	Coarse files	Band-leader Shaw		"Ah, me" / Uses scuba					Aura / Old-time cars					Curves / Reply: Abbr.				
Comic actor Alan						Tractor maker John						Puzzle / Overly sullen						
Barrel part						Im-passive							Not drunk					
Cone-bearing tree				___-ski	Takes away by force	Turf		Lily of Utah					WJM anchor Baxter	AMEX kin				
Wavers								Foster's river of song	Closed / Charged particle					Three or four	In an angry manner	Ford's prede-cessor	Ties up (the score)	Plant more grass
Sound of shock	Nile snakes	Tiff	Penny ante game	German toast							Oil worker / Wee bit							
				Sequoia / N.Z. bird								Infer						
Bike wheel parts						Karenina Lost utopia					Longing	Polishes Excused (from)						
Islama-bad's country									Peas' place	"So long!"			Dial sound					
Fret					Dance move Lament					Tidy up	Cost Widen a margin							
Marry	Fixes a manu-script	Kid / Eclair's kin				Lion-like Scarlet							Chem. bit			In the open	Range of hills	
			Leer	Pitching stat Went up				Lair				Ed Koch book						Verse
Hotel em-ployees								Opening letters	Take on Wind dir.						Bigwig Music's ___ Paul			
Not at all off-color												Ohio city						
Oral Roberts U. city					*Ghosts* writer							Come into sight						
Dutch painter Jan					Like a sachet								Goblet part					

BASKET CASE

Lettie Redhood has five doting relatives who live alone in cottages in the woods. One day she arranged to visit them all. Each of them (Aunt Laura, Aunt Lotta, Cousin Lila, Grandma Redhood, and Grandma Ryding) was so delighted that she promised Lettie a freshly baked goody. On the appointed day, Lettie set forth into the woods carrying her expectantly empty basket. It turned out, though, that the baked gifts were so large and heavy (one was an almond bundt cake) that she had to carry them home one at a time and set out anew for each subsequent cottage.

The map below shows the cottages (A through E) that Lettie visited and the only traversable paths through the woods. Given the map and the clues, can you identify the relative who lived in each cottage, the confection offered therein, and the order in which Lettie paid her visits?

ANSWER, PAGE 121

CLUES

1. Lettie visited both her grandmas—one of whom baked her an apple cobbler—before she visited her cousin.
2. As she trudged forth to pay her last visit, Lettie went to the right whenever she came to a fork in the path.
3. At the time she was putting the chocolate torte into her basket, she had already stowed Aunt Lotta's gift at home.
4. When Lettie arrived at one aunt's cottage, she had already received the fruitcake—but she had not yet taken the path to the right at the first fork upon entering the woods.
5. The cherry cheesecake was offered by neither of her aunts.
6. Lettie took more left forks to get to Grandma Ryding's cottage than she took to get to her other grandma's cottage.
7. The walk to Cousin Lila's cottage entailed choosing two consecutive left forks.

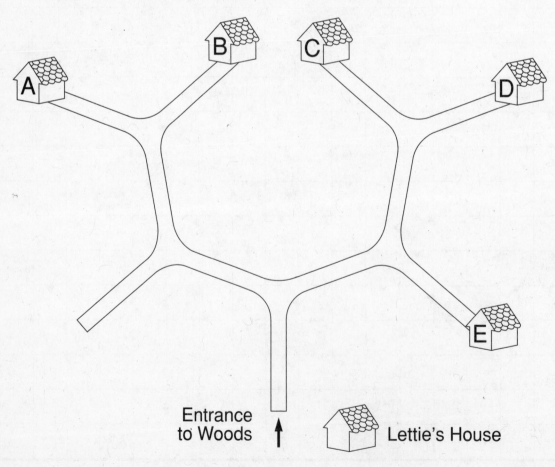

Entrance to Woods ↑   **Lettie's House**

DOUBLE CROSS 6

Directions appear on page 15.

ANSWER, PAGE 121

1E	2T	3A	4P	5V	■	6N	7H	8S	9U	■	10C	11M	12E	■	13F	14L	15B	16A	17D	18G	■ 19R 20O
21Q	22L	23K	■	24U	25C	26V	27J	■	28H	29A	30M	■	31Q	32S	33E	34G	35P	36L	■	37B	38I 39U 40T
41J	42D	43R	44H	■	45A	46V	47E	■	48N	49P	50M	51L	■	52O	53D	54R	■	55J	56F	■	57A 58E ■
59V	60C	61I	62P	■	63Q	64L	■	65G	66J	67M	68T	69U	70A	■	71N	72C	73P	74F	■	75S	■ 76Q 77L
78G	■	79O	80V	81I	82R	83B	84H	85A	86J	■	87M	■	88L	89C	90K	91S	■	92P	93F	94U	95A ■ 96N
97G	98V	99I	■	100E	101K	102P	■	103C	104Q	105D	106F	107S	■	108B	109U	110A	111E	■	112T	113G	■ 114P 115K
116V	■	117I	118M	119C	■	120Q	121E	122N	123A	■	124B	■	125L	126V	127D	■	128K	129F	130J	131E	■ 132A 133U
134C	135T	■	136I	137J	■	138B	139L	■	140R	141U	142D	■	143V	144B	145G	■	146K	147C	148P	■	149E 150O 151J
152M	153A	154H	155S	■	156F	157L	■	158E	159C	160K	■	161P	162G	163M	■	164I	165F	166A	167R	168E	■ 169G 170Q
171B	172O	■	173J	■	174P	175K	176U	■	177E	178T	179A	180H	■	181M	182V	183N	184F	■	■		

A. *The Wind in the Willows* author (2 wds.)
110 85 123 16 3 45 132 153 70 179 29 166 57 95

B. 1950s campaign slogan (3 wds.)
138 108 124 144 37 15 171 83

C. Colonist hanged as a spy in 1776 (2 wds.)
134 25 10 60 89 147 72 103 159 119

D. Eviscerated
17 53 105 42 142 127

E. Popular Thanksgiving dish (2 wds.)
100 33 58 47 1 149 12 131 158 177 121 111 168

F. Furnished with equipment
93 129 13 56 156 165 74 106 184

G. South African town under siege during the Boer War
169 34 78 145 18 65 97 113 162

H. Fully and unconditionally guaranteed
84 154 28 180 7 44

I. Wear out
61 38 99 81 136 164 117

J. Excessively grasping or covetous
86 27 137 66 41 173 55 151 130

K. Arabic for "gem of buildings" (2 wds.)
23 115 128 90 146 101 175 160

L. Partner of Sperry or Starsky
125 22 51 88 14 77 139 36 64 157

M. Main ingredient in meringue (2 wds.)
30 152 181 11 118 87 67 163 50

N. Bark
48 122 6 71 183 96

O. Push or jostle, in a way
172 150 20 52 79

P. *Christina's World* artist (2 wds.)
73 62 148 4 49 114 174 35 102 161 92

Q. Tending to peregrinate
63 21 120 31 76 170 104

R. Ripped bit of clothing
54 19 82 140 43 167

S. "What has four legs in the morning … ?" e.g.
8 75 107 155 32 91

T. Last of England's Henrys
40 112 135 2 68 178

U. Polite term substituting for an offensive one
69 133 39 141 9 24 109 176 94

V. American clockmaker, 1785-1859 (2 wds.)
116 5 98 46 59 80 182 26 126 143

OFF WITH THEIR HEADS!

ANSWER, PAGE 121

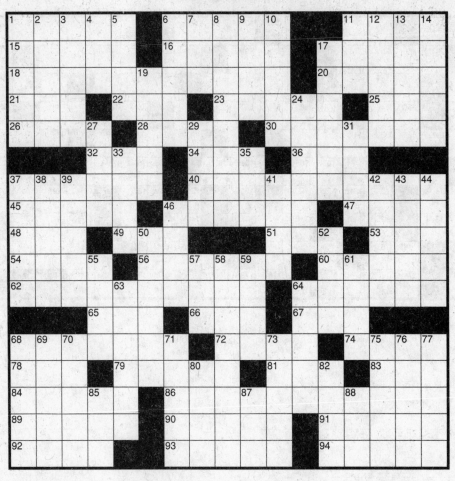

ACROSS

1 Consume entirely: 2 wds.
6 Social position
11 Llama's land
15 Stopped in one's tracks
16 "Poplar" ski resort
17 Missile homes
18 Sculler's woes?: 2 wds.
20 Singer Bryant
21 Suffix for journal or Japan
22 Smoker's concern
23 Hard to chew
25 Glutton
26 Turn to slush
28 Jazz background music
30 Wipeout of a sort
32 Dinghy propeller
34 Lend a hand
36 Before, to Burns
37 Blustering
40 Insult, perhaps?: 2 wds.
45 Tippy transport
46 Land of drachmas
47 Caddie's cry
48 Brigitte's buddy
49 Sault ___ Marie
51 Poetic pugilist
53 Summit
54 Nobelist Walesa
56 Kind of band, show, or army
60 Stockholm native
62 Sake?: 3 wds.
64 Sneaky fellow
65 Mauna ___
66 *Newhart* setting
67 Field judge
68 Recurring often
72 Olympic skater Thomas
74 Mary ___ Lincoln
78 Letters for debtors?
79 Without help
81 Songwriter Yoko
83 Kanga's kid, in *Winnie-the-Pooh*
84 Play the old banjo
86 It's usually where the squeak is: 2 wds.
89 Stop
90 Spiral-horned antelope
91 Here and there
92 ___ podrida (Spanish stew)
93 Sites for blotters
94 Full of fluff

DOWN

1 Stephanie Zimbalist's father
2 Got to one's feet
3 Target of some hotel thieves
4 Criminal's machine gun
5 Caged (up)
6 The Blue Grotto's island
7 Sly ___ fox: 2 wds.
8 Battle of Britain plane
9 "...a ___'clock scholar": 2 wds.
10 Follow
11 Wrestler's goal
12 Statesman Root
13 Copter part
14 Long-continued practice
17 African expanse
19 Cartoonist Trudeau
24 Hansel's sister
27 Matador's foe
29 Carnival
31 Feudal servant
33 Iowa campus town
35 Actor Billy ___ Williams
37 La ___ (Milan opera house)
38 Broken, as horses
39 In reserve: 2 wds.
41 Read over quickly
42 Carries
43 Wear down
44 Act anti-magnetically
46 Actress Rowlands
50 Where some Monopoly players are sent: 2 wds.
52 "Got it!": 2 wds.
55 Hawaiian port
57 Prefix with gram or center
58 South Africa's Winnie and Nelson
59 Henry VIII's Boleyn
61 Float gently
63 "A Horse With ___" (1972 hit): 2 wds.
64 Twist dry
68 The ___ Kid (Western hero)
69 Traveler's stop
70 Countrified
71 Babbled baby-talk
73 Some investments
75 Heavenly hunter
76 Cruller's kin
77 A bit bonkers
80 Aswan's river
82 October birthstone
85 "Born in the ___"
87 Squid's camouflage
88 Kimono sash

LIMBERICKS

A good limerick always ends with a twist, but a *limberick* ends every line with one. To solve, unscramble the five words given in capital letters to complete each verse. A good sense of pun helps.

ANSWERS, PAGE 120

1. BIRD CONTROL

"I was pecked by a bird I once WODEN,

So I'm scared of the seagulls," she DANGERO.

To impress her, her ABUE

Threw some rocks at each COWR

And made sure to leave *no* tern DUSENNOT.

2. HAIR RAID

The fellow, perversely SEBSODES

With producing more hair on his SHECT,

Transplants, he MISTAD,

The hair from his ZIPTS,

Leaving Fido completely "STRISEDDES."

3. OUT OF ORDER

In Parliament, students from HOSSLOC

Were ejected for acting like LOSFO.

The law there BITHISPOR

Outsiders who BITIZK,

And Britannia does not waive the LUSER.

RICK TULKA

CRYPTIC CROSSWORD 1

Each clue in a cryptic crossword contains two parts: a definition of the answer and a second description of it through wordplay. Finding the dividing point between parts is the key to solving.

Watch for anagrams, hidden words, charades of two or more smaller words, and other language tricks.

ANSWER, PAGE 121

ACROSS

1 Refuse to accept Twisted Sister (6)

4 Hurry up, playing set point (4,2,2)

9 Capone and Eisenhower must be similar (5)

10 Wrongly called for end of program, interrupting TV's talking horse (9)

11 Past … past … past … past harbor of Samoa (4,4)

12 Slinky character with painter's prop (6)

14 The first man makes a home for beavers (4)

15 Worshipper's marriage vow: "Some other time" (8)

19 Nun keeping in dark (8)

20 Returned newsmagazine issue (4)

23 Cyril's new poems (6)

25 Negative reply about mean video game maker (8)

27 Handcuffing guy with a grip (9)

28 Blueprint includes one level area (5)

29 Crop chewed up by one ass (8)

30 Attempt to keep burnt remains like garbage (6)

DOWN

1 Show up again to harvest fruit (8)

2 Small cans containing dull-colored fish (9)

3 Inattentive Confederate general captured by agent (6)

5 Throw to shortstop (4)

6 Offers writhing serpents (8)

7 Phone book listings for northern Iowa city (5)

8 Get odd letters admitting stroll (6)

10 Big serving of English pop-rock coming up (8)

13 Changing triangle all around (8)

16 Reagan's concealing passion for Europeans (9)

17 Dad's brother catches cold in vehicle (8)

18 Lawyer in a contest of jousting verbally (8)

21 Article carried by little climbing beasts of Peru (6)

22 Proust novel induces trance (6)

24 Long-limbed, angry alien (5)

26 One cat among millions (4)

BY RICHARD MARSH

ALPHABET CITY

Besides being the capital of Texas, Austin happens to have the largest population of any American city whose name begins with the letter A. How many of the largest U.S. cities beginning with each of the other 25 letters of the alphabet can you name? Our source: the 1990 U.S. census.

ANSWERS AND RATINGS, PAGE 122

A USTIN

B

C

D

E

F

G

H

I

J

K

L

M

N

O

P

Q

R

S

T

U

V

W

X

Y

Z

JUMBO CROSSWORD 2

ANSWER, PAGE 122

ACROSS

1 Loose-fitting smock
7 Portrays
14 Join forces: 2 wds.
20 Maker of amends
21 Cancellation due to weather
22 Queued up: 2 wds.
23 Planet-bound probe
24 Walt Disney World location
25 Salad maker
26 Shopper's "gift": 2 wds.
28 Bible seamstress
30 Pouch
31 Location
32 Rams
33 *Deutschlander*'s language
34 Ceremony
35 VCR remote button
37 Photographer's accessories
38 Commonest craps roll
39 Dunderhead
42 Wee bits
44 Ignoring morals
46 Pays attention to
48 Tiffany rival
50 Roy's pardner
51 Botching the play
53 Of the shoulder
55 Bribe
59 Israel's Tel ___
60 The Lorelei's river
62 Sky diver, for example
64 Agent Orange, e.g.
66 Los Angeles squad
68 Cockney's champion
69 Started an extinguished cigarette
70 Proclaims
71 Rowing team
72 Heckler's sound
75 Charged the account of
76 Trim the topiary
77 Everybody else
78 Brought to a point
79 Less snug
80 Putting place
81 Concealed
82 Short-legged hounds
83 His ___ (important person)
84 Curtail
85 Tracks down
86 Application form question
87 Evaded duties
88 Poker cheat
92 Mountebank
94 Dish served "con carne"
95 Friend to Françoise
96 Sign of a bad window washer
97 Stick shift setting: 2 wds.
100 Khomeini, for one
102 Opposite of *sans*
104 Uncle Remus character: 2 wds.
106 Hymn accompaniment
107 Blind alley
111 Virtually: 2 wds.
113 CIA's predecessor
114 Ours: 2 wds., Fr.
115 Preferences
117 Refrain syllables
119 Red light meaning
120 Flooding preventers
121 Boutique
122 Track circuits
126 Felix or Fritz
127 Matador
128 *Jeopardy!* host: 2 wds.
130 Protein-forming acids
132 Swindle
134 Dawn goddess
135 Indicate
136 Dante subject
137 Feel in one's bones
138 More irritable
139 Reserve cash: 2 wds.
140 Get comfy

DOWN

1 ___ liver (meat purchase)
2 Pioneer video game company
3 Impressionist Claude
4 Over one's head: 2 wds.
5 Envisions
6 Printing goof
7 Intimated, in a way: 3 wds.
8 Viscount's superiors
9 Hoard
10 "___ pig's eye!": 2 wds.
11 Electrical capacitor
12 Henry VIII and Elizabeth I
13 Made a sudden attack on
14 American ICBM
15 Baseballer Slaughter
16 Capp and Pacino
17 Letter
18 Like leftovers
19 Hundredth part
27 Orchestra output
29 Studied before robbing
33 Bottled spirit
34 Strong rotgut
36 Org.
37 "___ Entertain You": 2 wds.
38 Light lunches
39 Leading
40 Start the match
41 Letter stroke
43 Infantryman in Nam
45 Flavoring buds
47 Some exes
49 Glowed
52 Gives the third degree
54 Served the soup
56 Cause of wear and tear
57 Safety equipment at a three-alarm blaze: 2 wds.
58 Pinks and roses
61 Call the cabbie
63 Comic Foxx
65 Ascertain
66 Chided
67 Out of bed
70 Goddess of sorcery
71 Line in a gun sight: 2 wds.
72 French brandies
73 Where this puzzle's grid is located: 2 wds.
74 Smokey ___: 2 wds.
75 Keyhole place, at times
76 Mails
78 Like some perfumes
79 *Coming to America* director John
81 Voucher
82 Folk singer Ives
84 Burger joint orders
85 Questionable hangover cure: 4 wds.
87 Works like a horse
88 Wheat waste
89 Friend to Fernando
90 Moreno and Hayworth
91 Hammer ends
93 Become well-informed (with "on"): 2 wds.
94 Largest of the asteroids
98 Charitable contributions, e.g.
99 Heredity deciders
101 ___ *Baltimore* (Norman Lear show)
103 Supply the eats for
105 Noted copier company
107 Waterfall
108 Wild
109 Getting the spoils of war
110 Collapsed: 2 wds.
112 Kangaroo, e.g.
116 Peaceful
118 Warns
120 Also-ran
121 Threw
123 Nearby
124 Jeopardy
125 Emulate Hans Brinker
127 Lug
128 Bern's river
129 Scandinavian character
131 Public Enemy ___: 2 wds.
133 No longer working: Abbr.

NOT ALL THERE

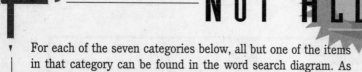

For each of the seven categories below, all but one of the items in that category can be found in the word search diagram. As usual, answers may read horizontally, vertically, or diagonally, always in a straight line. And no answer word is hidden entirely within another. (For example, if both WORD and SWORDPLAY were hidden, WORD could be found somewhere other than within SWORDPLAY.) Once you've determined which member of a category is not found in the grid, write its name on the blank provided. The first letters of these unaccounted-for members will spell an appropriate word.

ANSWER, PAGE 122

```
T Y E L L O W H B L U E E R F S
N E A R E Y C I T N A L T A E L
O Y S U M M E R N R T R W M U E
S I Z S R S I A T T N C C K G E
K S O E M A H H N O E E T G P
C V T J E A N H A T T R Y N I Y
A I O U P N M U T U A U A R R C
J O F P E M S M S L D R E U M S
O L Y I K R A M U P O B C E A R
H E N T C J O F N T C R S T H H
N T A E O A H M E K E E U S I A
P E A R R S P A V M G R E E N C
E T S L A D D R H E N T E E M K
P R O B E R T S E Y E P O D S T
```

Find: **Not There:**

3 of the 4 Gospel writers of the New Testament .... _____

6 of the 7 colors of the rainbow .... _____

5 of the 6 actresses who played Angels on *Charlie's Angels*

  (last names only) .... _____

3 of the 4 seasons of the year .... _____

4 of the 5 oceans of the world .... _____

8 of the 9 planets of our solar system .... _____

6 of the 7 Dwarfs .... _____

1.

2.

3.

4.

BATHDAY WISH

ANSWER, PAGE 122

ACROSS

1 Beatnik's homes
5 Scotch partner
9 Comes up to hit
13 ___ a time: 2 wds.
15 Movie star, often
16 Thessaly peak
18 Start of an Andy Rooney quote: 4 wds.
20 Let up
21 "The heat ___!": 2 wds.
22 Part 2 of the quote: 2 wds.
24 Rank below corp.
26 "Star Wars," initially
28 Scratches out a living
29 Federal Express competitor
30 Sad sacks' sacks
32 Patty Hearst's kidnappers: Abbr.
34 Working hard: 2 wds.
36 Part 3 of the quote: 4 wds.
40 "That's awful!"
43 Dadaism founder
44 Cole Porter's "Let's ___ ": 2 wds.
45 Michael Caine title role
47 Third-largest African nation
50 Draft org.
51 Lunchtimes
52 Perform well
53 Osso ___ (Italian veal entree)
54 Genetic double helix
55 Originally called
56 Part 4 of the quote: 3 wds.
62 Battle between clans
63 French diarist Anaïs
64 Father a foal
65 Pebble Beach prop
67 Year-end closeout
70 Mr. Sheep
72 Collar
73 Part 5 of the quote: 2 wds.
76 Col. Potter's unit, on TV
78 Become successful
79 End of the quote: 3 wds.
83 Member of many clubs
84 A percentage (of)
85 Thriller writer John Le ___
86 Milwaukee product
87 Buffalo's lake
88 Chew like a beaver

DOWN

1 Luau food
2 Not to mention
3 Corpus ___
4 Je ne ___ quoi (elusive quality)
5 Get off your feet
6 Skunk's defense
7 Maynard's friend, on old TV
8 "Smart" guy
9 "How have you ___ ?"
10 Thoroughgoing, as an effort
11 Traffic jam
12 Jukebox selections
16 "Abracadabra!"
17 Ultimate degee
19 Finishes: 2 wds.
23 Candy box's shape
24 Desktop publishers' IBMs
25 Egg ___ yung
27 Home sick
31 Throw a fright into
33 Makes sense: 2 wds.
35 "___ Be Loved by You": 2 wds.
37 Bully's threat: 2 wds.
38 1900 Puccini opera
39 "He doesn't know ___ strength": 2 wds.
40 Night light, of sorts
41 Tom Collins base
42 "___ So Fine" (1963 Chiffons hit)
46 Lies in a hammock
47 Meditative sect
48 Paul Bunyan's tool
49 Water cooler?
53 Untalented with: 2 wds.
54 Hard worker
57 Coup action
58 Televise
59 Small-time, as a gambler
60 Stat for Seaver
61 Civil War soldier
62 Catty?
65 Go pitapat
66 Supernatural
68 Rental agreement
69 Annoying computer word
71 Painter Chagall
73 ___ Mahal
74 Endlessly
75 Trucker's rig
77 Unexpected problem
80 Lilliputian
81 "___ Lippo Lippi" (Browning poem)
82 Not very many

DOUBLE CROSS 7

Directions appear on page 15.

ANSWER, PAGE 122

1F	2R	3L	4O	5P		6Q	7F		8X	9M		10X	11Q	12R	13F	14H		15R	16J	17G
18L		19A	20X	21I	22K		23U	24D	25Q	26T		27J	28B		29I	30X	31H		32G	33C
34A	35B		36A	37U		38W	39H	40G	41T	42R		43A	44L		45W	46D	47S		48S	49V
50M	51F		52U	53A	54J	55W		56Q	57B	58I	59P		60S	61K		62O	63H	64T		65K
66P	67B	68W	69T	70X	71N	72S	73O	74J	75L	76U		77O	78N		79H	80X	81J	82E	83M	84Q
85A	86L	87P		88H	89T	90S	91E	92Q		93F	94A	95S	96V		97H	98O		99A	100S	101O
102E		103I	104E	105R	106P	107M	108H	109B	110L	111F	112C	113O	114A		115K	116S	117C	118I		119A
120B	121H		122H	123V	124E		125C	126U	127H	128D	129N	130F	131A		132R	133W	134H	135J	136W
137F	138R		139V	140O	141L		142R	143M	144C	145U		146E	147R	148N	149K		150H	151M	152R
153R	154N	155Q	156X	157S	158I	159H	160K	161G	162D	163M	164E								

A. Ross Perot or Donald Trump
$\overline{19}\ \overline{36}\ \overline{94}\ \overline{53}\ \overline{43}\ \overline{99}\ \overline{34}\ \overline{119}\ \overline{85}$
$\overline{114}\ \overline{131}$

B. Anger, as by an insult
$\overline{57}\ \overline{67}\ \overline{28}\ \overline{109}\ \overline{120}\ \overline{35}$

C. Recurring theme
$\overline{144}\ \overline{117}\ \overline{112}\ \overline{33}\ \overline{125}$

D. Helmut Kohl's capital
$\overline{162}\ \overline{24}\ \overline{46}\ \overline{128}$

E. International understanding
$\overline{104}\ \overline{102}\ \overline{146}\ \overline{164}\ \overline{82}\ \overline{91}\ \overline{124}$

F. Gilligan, for one
$\overline{130}\ \overline{93}\ \overline{7}\ \overline{1}\ \overline{137}\ \overline{13}\ \overline{111}\ \overline{51}$

G. City near Chernobyl
$\overline{32}\ \overline{161}\ \overline{40}\ \overline{17}$

H. 1964 Beatles movie (4 wds.)
$\overline{159}\ \overline{39}\ \overline{150}\ \overline{127}\ \overline{121}\ \overline{88}\ \overline{97}\ \overline{31}\ \overline{79}$
$\overline{14}\ \overline{134}\ \overline{108}\ \overline{63}\ \overline{122}$

I. Noisy commotion
$\overline{21}\ \overline{158}\ \overline{118}\ \overline{58}\ \overline{29}\ \overline{103}$

J. Candy bar center
$\overline{135}\ \overline{27}\ \overline{54}\ \overline{81}\ \overline{16}\ \overline{74}$

K. Kind-hearted, as a barman?
$\overline{160}\ \overline{22}\ \overline{61}\ \overline{115}\ \overline{149}\ \overline{65}$

L. Blot on the landscape
$\overline{86}\ \overline{18}\ \overline{3}\ \overline{44}\ \overline{75}\ \overline{110}\ \overline{141}$

M. Meat- or cheese-filled pasta
$\overline{151}\ \overline{143}\ \overline{50}\ \overline{107}\ \overline{9}\ \overline{163}\ \overline{83}$

N. French painter of *Le Déjeuner sur l'herbe*
$\overline{148}\ \overline{129}\ \overline{154}\ \overline{71}\ \overline{78}$

O. Modern novel's protagonist
$\overline{73}\ \overline{98}\ \overline{62}\ \overline{77}\ \overline{140}\ \overline{101}\ \overline{4}\ \overline{113}$

P. Dinner held on the first night of Passover
$\overline{87}\ \overline{5}\ \overline{59}\ \overline{66}\ \overline{106}$

Q. Sheer party dress fabric
$\overline{155}\ \overline{92}\ \overline{6}\ \overline{84}\ \overline{56}\ \overline{25}\ \overline{11}$

R. 1932 Pulitzer-winning Gershwin musical (4 wds.)
$\overline{12}\ \overline{105}\ \overline{138}\ \overline{2}\ \overline{152}\ \overline{42}\ \overline{147}\ \overline{142}\ \overline{153}$
$\overline{15}\ \overline{132}$

S. Scrooge's chief trait
$\overline{100}\ \overline{90}\ \overline{72}\ \overline{95}\ \overline{60}\ \overline{157}\ \overline{116}\ \overline{48}\ \overline{47}$

T. Comforter material
$\overline{89}\ \overline{69}\ \overline{26}\ \overline{64}\ \overline{41}$

U. Temporary memory space in a computer
$\overline{52}\ \overline{126}\ \overline{23}\ \overline{37}\ \overline{145}\ \overline{76}$

V. Inaugural day event
$\overline{96}\ \overline{49}\ \overline{139}\ \overline{123}$

W. Sandinista leader Daniel
$\overline{133}\ \overline{68}\ \overline{38}\ \overline{55}\ \overline{136}\ \overline{45}$

X. Now-friendly alien, in *Star Trek: The Next Generation*
$\overline{10}\ \overline{20}\ \overline{80}\ \overline{8}\ \overline{70}\ \overline{156}\ \overline{30}$

"C" HERE

Fill in the 74 words below (each of which contains one or more C's) so that they interlock in standard crisscross fashion in the grid. When the puzzle is completed, each word will be used exactly once. A starting hint appears on the bottom left corner of page 127.

ANSWER, PAGE 122

3 LETTERS
ACE
CAT
COB
COD
COO
COY
CUB
CUE

4 LETTERS
CAPE
CHIC
COOK
CUTE

EPIC
ETCH
KICK
LACE
NICE
PICA
SECT
TACK
TALC

5 LETTERS
CAMEO
CHIME
COCOA

CREDO
CREEK
DECAL
EXCEL
NIECE
OCCUR
SCALE
SLICE
TRACE
UNCLE

6 LETTERS
ACACIA
ACCEDE
ACIDIC

CATTLE
CHANCE
CHOICE
CLERIC
CLEVER
CLOCHE
CLUTCH
CRITIC
CROCUS
DOCKET
NICKEL
POCKET
SOCCER
TACKLE

7 LETTERS
ARCHAIC
COCONUT
CONCERN
CONCERT
CRACKER
CRUNCHY
CRYBABY
PACIFIC
SUCCESS
TUSSOCK

8 LETTERS
BACKPACK
CATCHALL

CHARCOAL
CHEERFUL
CLEMENCY
ECLECTIC
LIMERICK

9 LETTERS
ACOUSTICS
BLACKJACK
CLASSICAL
COINCIDED
CONESTOGA
RECOLLECT

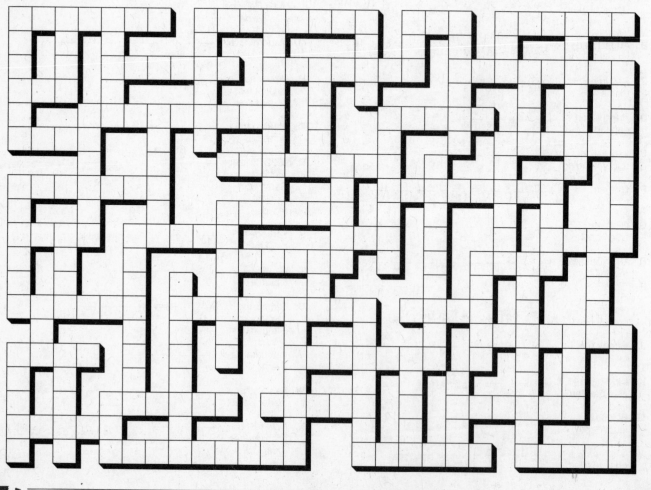

PENCIL POINTERS 6

In this crossword the clues appear in the grid itself. Enter the answers in the direction of the pointers.

ANSWER, PAGE 123

The grid contains the following clues:

- Stephen King book
- Singer Guthrie
- Olympic luge, for example
- Started a golf hole
- Catch sight of
- On the agenda
- ___ Gay (WW2 bomber)
- Female graduate
- Ousted from power
- Ugly sight
- Spur on
- Like serious plays
- Didn't do anything
- Put ___ to (finish)
- Studious geeks
- ___ and crafts
- Fleetness
- Person to follow
- Charles's queen-to-be
- Perry Mason's creator
- Get some shut-eye
- "Rug"
- Wide-awake
- St. ___ Fire
- "Neither rain nor snow ..."
- Patches up
- Poorly made
- Pagan practice
- Comfort
- Goatee setting
- Long, long time
- Cheers star Ted
- Annexes
- Year-end paycheck extra
- Girls with an uncle
- Capital of Norway
- Flying-related: Prefix
- Feats in horseshoes
- Jules Verne character
- Feds
- Hamlet, for one
- Boise's state
- Name of the Rose author
- Sleuth Spade
- Reckless courage
- Inquisitive nature
- Butterfly catching aid
- Initials for a hit show
- The Red Planet
- The ___ Cometh
- Pot stake
- Narrow valley
- Tribe member
- Lofty talk
- Bill of fare
- Cave
- Causes chemical change
- Tailor's aids
- Aussie's returning weapon
- Folding money
- Changed
- Common brownie additive
- Rich cake
- Car's MPG raters
- Ship of 1492
- Early English invaders
- Issued a challenge
- Family Ties mother
- Period of history
- Animal's mouth
- Clothing joints
- Used a stool
- Sing to one's sweetie
- Cleo's killer
- Fashion designer Bill
- Fizzy beverage
- Branch of math, for short
- Of the backbone
- Guerrilla leader Guevara
- Mini-mally
- Health resort
- Fit to be tied
- Bob Cratchit's son
- One-time D.C. ball team
- Bro's sibling
- Pub orders
- Prism's rainbow effect
- Dunks
- Las Vegas's state
- Pastoral poem
- Piled up
- Painter Édouard
- Superior to
- Onset
- Aliens, for short
- Once more
- Strikes from copy
- Past, present, or future
- Borders
- Choir voice
- Inside info
- Lech Walesa, for one
- Mother of Castor & Pollux
- Calm
- Border on
- Pigpen
- Fill with horror: Var.
- Lassie or Benji
- Bothered
- Writer Ephron et al.
- Pillaged
- "Git ___, little dogie"
- Tennis great Chris
- City of Ohio or Spain
- Tightly packed
- Irritable
- Aïda viewing aid

FOR MYSTERY LOVERS

This diagramless is 21 squares wide by 21 squares deep and has left-to-right symmetry. As a hint, the location of the starting square is given on the bottom right corner of page 127.

ANSWER, PAGE 123

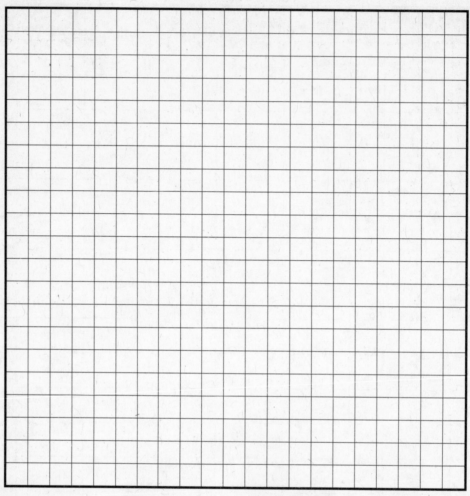

ACROSS

1 Smile warmly
5 Couch
9 Goldbricked
11 Tennis infractions
13 Interrogation formats?: 2 wds.
18 Mongrels
19 Linger
20 Bides one's time
22 Venice's Bridge of ___
23 Oft-candied tuber
24 Measles signs
26 *Bus Stop* playwright
27 Bedframe part
28 His VP was RMN
29 100 yrs.
32 ___ long way toward: 2 wds.
35 Airport schedule abbr.
36 Foul up
37 French pre-Impressionist painter
39 Barry Manilow's first hit
41 Sister Bertrille, e.g.
42 School for priests: Abbr.
43 Villainous Vader
44 Homeric epic
45 Barbie's beau
46 Greek cross
47 Flight unit
48 Feeds the hogs
49 "What was ___ do?": 2 wds.
50 Nervous
52 Unending
54 Q-V link
55 A square ___ a round hole: 2 wds.
57 Church officers
58 Goes up
59 Give new cushioning to
61 Dark, full-bodied ale
62 Charles's princedom
63 Varnish ingredient
65 Continental abbr.
66 Assistants
67 Time of the crime?: 3 wds.
72 Neighbor of Saudi Arabia
73 Stage instruction
74 Fit for a king
76 Poe bird
77 Pilot's test cockpit
79 "___ awesome, fer shurr!"
80 Answer
81 Secret agent

DOWN

1 Fleet members
2 Dumbo's "wings"
3 Toward the stern
4 Fulfilled, as obligations
5 With 6-Down, wouldn't dance
6 See 5-Down
7 Imperfection
8 Book of maps
9 Mythical river of amnesia
10 Morse code component
11 Sauté
12 Omits
13 The culprit?
14 Stable staple
15 Cenozoic, for one
16 Sleeve filler
17 The booty?: 2 wds.
18 Mentalist: 2 wds.
21 Small sculptures
22 Dodge
25 Of tin
29 Raccoon relative
30 Quick business trip
31 Bulletins
32 Lionhearted
33 Liver companion
34 Make adjustments
37 LPs' successors
38 Be menacing
39 Where "Show Me" is the motto
40 Trios of feet: Abbr.
51 Cries of alarm
53 Tonto's horse
54 Poet James Whitcomb
56 Discourteous
58 Gary Burghoff role, on *M*A*S*H*
60 Jacques Cousteau, for one
62 Make broader
64 Titles
66 Autumn bloom
68 On the up-and-up
69 Sweep off one's feet
70 Without a mess
71 Diplomat
75 Troubadours' instruments
76 Come from behind to win
78 Scandinavian nomad

SIAMESE TWINS

This puzzle gives you two grids for the price of one. And two sets of clues to go with them, so you can work both crosswords at the same time. What's the catch? Each clue number is followed by two different clues to two different answers. The puzzle is to figure out which answer goes in which grid. The answers to 1-Across have been filled in. *ANSWERS, PAGE 123*

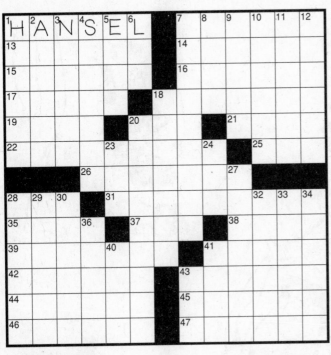

Grid 1: H A N S E L (1-Across)

Grid 2: G R E T E L (1-Across)

ACROSS

1 Woodland wanderer … / … and his sister
7 Model's work / Dan's anchoring predecessor
13 *Lawrence of Arabia* star / Take away
14 First poker bettor / Philippines seaport
15 Plays a banjo / Evolutionary missing links
16 *Bonanza* setting / Position
17 Rotates / Breath mint brand
18 Being risked: 2 wds. / Took the wheel
19 Oklahoma city / *Othello* villain
20 That ship / Weapon
21 Rani's gown / Sign of things to come
22 Basic / AWOL ones
25 Point opposite NNW / Begleys, Sr. and Jr.
26 Letter start: 2 wds. / Parodies
28 Speedy jet / Fly trap
31 Determination of a ship's position / Trashy book: 2 wds.
35 Therefore / Unevenly balanced
37 Capp and Capone / Scoundrel
38 Rare individual / Composer Bartók
39 Thornton Wilder play: 2 wds. / Go off course
41 Donut's shape / Desperado chaser
42 Show plainly / Canadian capital
43 Translate a cipher / Author Truman
44 Apartment dweller / Block-and-tackle part
45 Amends maker / Spotted American wildcat
46 Golfers J. C. and Sam / Ignores the posted limit
47 Passover feasts / Go around again, on the highway

DOWN

1 George's comic wife / Emceed
2 Bring into harmony / Cancel, as a law
3 Action star Chuck / Come in view
4 Played a note on / Native drums
5 Nights before holidays / Shade trees
6 ___ *Misérables* / Actor Cariou
7 They're stamped on stamps / 1935 Maxwell Anderson play
8 Out of the wind / Chooses
9 Absolutely adores / Old treaty org.
10 Beauty pageant crowns / ___ only (just by title): 2 wds.
11 Smooched / Church officers
12 Rock tour worker / Salad ingredients
18 News story / Atlanta-burning general
20 Some flights / Aardvarks and pangolins
23 Corn helping / Crimson
24 MGM mascot / Sermon subject
27 Was nosy / 1987 Peter Weller movie
28 Small porches / Tall boots for fishermen
29 Football team / "Hush!": 2 wds.
30 Slow critter / Of cows
32 Shoe cushion / Home of Shakespeare's gentlemen
33 Wise counselor of Greek myth / Gives the slip to
34 Welcomes / Space age weapons
36 Ship of 1492 / Like week-old bread
40 Had debts / Scored with the serve
41 Frenchman's head / Gait
43 Popular TV comedian, for short / Women's patriotic org.

BY DICK GAUTIER

PAIRAGRAMS

Whoever *loves* to solve anagrams will find this puzzle a snap. Each of the 12 pictures below is a "Pairagram," which can be described by two words containing the same letters in different order. For example, the first picture represents a NORSE SNORE. The lengths of the answers are indicated by the number of dashes. How many can you get?

ANSWERS, PAGE 122

1. N O R S E
    S N O R E

2. _ _ _ _ _ _
    _ _ _ _ _ _

3. _ _ _ _ _ _ , _
    _ _ _ _ _ _

4. _ _ _ _ _ _ _ _
    _ _ _ _ _ _ _ _

5. _ _ _ _ _ _
    _ _ _ _ _ _

6. _ _ _ _ _ _ _ _

_ _ _ _ _ _ _ _

7. _ _ _ _ _ _ _

8. _ _ _ _ _ _ _ _ _

_ _ _ _ _ _ _ _ _

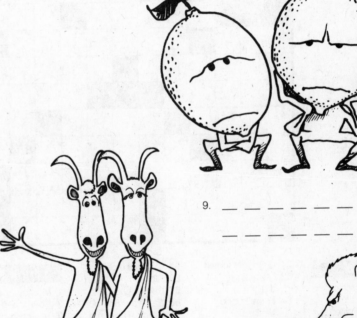

9. _ _ _ _ _ _ _

_ _ _ _ _ _ _

10. _ _ _ _ _ _

_ _ _ _ _ _

11. _ _ _ _ _ _ _ ,

_ _ _ _ _ _

12. _ _ _ _ _ _ _ _ _

_ _ _ _ _ _ _ _ _

ANYTOWN, USA

ANSWER, PAGE 123

ACROSS

1 Jellied mold
6 Secret plot
11 Keep, editorially
15 PC cursor control
16 Girlfriend: It.
17 Actress Shire
19 "Neato!"
20 Orioles' team doc?: 2 wds.
22 Accessory for a cat or a cow
24 Cable connection, e.g.
25 Central, for short
26 Blessing from Oral Roberts University?: 2 wds.
29 The picture of health?
30 *Return of the ___*
31 Gold, to Gomez
32 "Amazing" magician
34 Tennille and Morrison
35 British rainwear
37 Law offices
39 "I ___ Hold Your Hand": 2 wds.
40 Run away, in a way
42 Guest
44 Thesaurus entry: Abbr.
45 Up ___ (in trouble): 2 wds.
47 Tawdry
49 Mr. Turkey
52 "... but also to suffer for ___" (Phil. 1:29): 2 wds.
54 Kitchenwares item
58 Made smooth
60 Prom dress material
62 Pivot
63 "___ rip!": 2 wds.
64 Original hippies
66 Moo goo ___ pan
67 Part of Q.E.D.
68 *Elephant Boy* boy
71 Proof of age in a western capital?: 2 wds.
73 Guy's companion
74 Men of Mexico
76 Sign with a shine?
77 Loudspeaker for a Billy Joel song?: 2 wds.
80 Hurry
83 Irish county
84 Actress Moore and others
85 "___-loo-ra-loo-ral ..."
86 Garbage vessel
87 Paradisiacal places
88 Variety

DOWN

1 Morns, for short
2 Boar's pen pal?
3 Top military man on a reservation?: 2 wds.
4 Polynesian getaways
5 Basement
6 Bandleader Calloway
7 Nepalese nanny
8 First draft from a Gulf town?: 2 wds.
9 Thespian
10 First dog in space
11 "Whoa!"
12 Street surface
13 Periodic table items
14 Shyness
18 Willis's role on *Moonlighting*
21 Very, to Valdez
23 Bread purchase
26 Heavy volume
27 River to the Caspian
28 Cutlery
30 Singer Bon Jovi
33 Most arid
34 ___ *Bulba* (Yul Brynner film)
36 Baden-Baden, for one
38 Wheat-cutting tool
39 Sadness
41 Old-time anesthesia
43 "I was working in ___ late one night ..." ("Monster Mash"): 2 wds.
46 Banish
48 Cherry's center
49 Russian carts
50 Farmer's garb
51 Tinny, e.g.
53 Down East coroner?: 2 wds.
55 Hospital room in the Beaver state?: 2 wds.
56 True: Fr.
57 Actress Markey
59 Take-home
61 Harrow's rival
65 Nap
68 Word after ready
69 Battery terminal
70 Gave in (to)
72 Sleepiness
74 Winter fall
75 Whirl
78 Self
79 Lamebrain
81 N.O.W. goal
82 It breaks every morning

DOUBLE CROSS 8

Directions appear on page 15.

1F	2B		3O	4U	5R		6G	7C		8M	9P	10K	11B	12V	13O		14M	15A	16I	17G	18D
19N	20F	21W		22L	23X	24A	25P	26B	27T	28V	29S		30W	31X	32E	33M	34H	35C	36I	37O	38N
39D	40F	41S	42U		43L	44B	45N	46A	47W	48G		49V	50F	51B	52T	53J	54Q	55R	56C	57L		58C
59S	60X	61B	62F	63O	64K	65A		66M	67D	68N	69U	70W		71R	72T	73B	74V		75P	76Q	77J	78E
79T	80F	81S	82D	83A		84W	85H	86A		87S	88V	89F	90B	91I	92H	93C	94P		95O	96U	97V
98K	99N		100M	101U	102E	103O	104R		105G	106B	107O	108I	109K	110C	111M	112Q	113V	114H		115E	116D
117B	118K	119J		120C	121A	122V	123W	124K	125F	126U		127K	128A	129N		130T	131I	132B	133O	134Q		135N
136X	137S	138D	139V	140E	141B	142J	143O		144W	145N		146F	147P	148C	149O	150N	151S	152D		153D	154S
155X	156G	157Q	158O	159P	160M	161F	162W		163S	164X	165G		166H	167R	168U		169T	170J		171T	172I
173A		174R	175N	176P	177C	178L	179K		180M	181Q		182V	183S	184L	185M	186U	187K	188C	189T		

A. Precipitation precipitator? (2 wds.)
121 173 46 15 86 128 65 24 83

B. Conspicuously showy
11 2 106 44 26 117 73 132 141 61 90 51

C. Site of Pickett's charge
110 35 120 56 188 7 58 93 148 177

D. Unrestrained, as praise
152 39 116 138 18 153 82 67

E. Annual event in Prescott, Arizona
102 115 140 78 32

F. Gateway to Afghanistan (2 wds.)
62 20 161 50 125 40 89 1 146 80

G. A soft one "turneth away wrath"
6 48 105 17 165 156

H. Refined, as one's skills
166 92 85 34 114

I. "Bean"
131 16 108 36 91 172

J. Sacher Hotel specialty
77 170 53 142 119

K. The Great Compromiser (2 wds.)
118 187 109 179 64 127 124 98 10

L. Magazine founded by John Harold Johnson in 1945
178 43 184 22 57

M. Galaxy's core, theoretically (2 wds.)
66 185 8 33 14 111 180 160 100

N. Religious investiture
175 129 38 68 99 135 19 150 145 45

O. Max Theiler developed the vaccine for this (2 wds.)
143 37 103 63 158 95 3 13 149 133 107

P. Shut out
94 25 147 9 159 75 176

Q. Setting for the Inspector Morse mysteries
157 76 181 112 134 54

R. When the rabbi slept late
71 5 55 174 167 104

S. Across ___, E. L. Masters's autobiography (2 wds.)
137 87 41 163 154 59 81 151 29 183

T. Describing radioactive isotopes
52 79 189 169 27 171 72 130

U. Former Burmese capital, site of 730 pagodas
42 96 69 168 4 186 101 126

V. "When it rains it pours" (2 wds.)
28 88 139 182 122 12 97 49 113 74

W. Moussaka ingredient
21 47 70 30 123 84 162 144

X. It's best when blue
31 23 136 155 60 164

BY ROBERT LEIGHTON
DSZQUPHSBNT! 2
Directions appear on page 38.

ANSWERS, PAGE 123

1. CRYPTOON

VZFR IGMVW! OJR VZGEYR
OJPO AMA KZ HPAYS ZT
"*OJR *TRCYSCRA *BPFR"
MK TZC ZT "*AMQZXVR
*VZGXO!"

2. QUITE A LIKENESS

"FCQNQ PL K NQKLHE
ZQHZDQ DHHS FCQ JKR
FCQR UH. FCQ AKGQ HEQ
JQKNL CKL TQQE
QKNEQU FCNHMXC
ZQNLQOQNKEGQ."—*KD
*CPNLGCAQDU

3. SO LONG, AGO

LYK LKIG "PAAS-MDK" RWV
KLDGANAPBEWNND
RYBLLNKS SARZ UIAG LYK
AZK-LBGK UWIKRKNN
"*PAS MK RBLY DK."

4. SIMPLE DEDUCTION

*YUTKWBQA, TEDJFXFXN
TJHVG NKDLT, VTWWY
*SDVYBX, "VUTKT'Y DX
CXOTKUDXOTO
CXOTKVDATK CXOTKIBBV—
CXOTKYVDXO?"

5. STICK UP

GCYL RYILNW ANWWYM ILB
KYDDQ WMNXUF XEDDSBYB,
ELY BMSPYM FCENWYB,
"CYDR VY TYW ENW EJ WCSF
KIV!" WCY MYRDQ:"SL I KSJ!"

6. GLUG, GLUG

TVHTXRW TXKBNXN JTMJ
CFZ-JXTDCTCX WTGNNG
JXTGXNI FHX JZRPPRCDBM,
XFFU T IREN, ZNCX IFZC
XKN IGTRC.

7. ENVIRONMENTAL WARNING

LHZMP PHZZV MHZMI,
PDVMG WZQYL HMRZV,
OQLAP BCIZP KQPMF
DRDYZ FMGZH FMPZH,
VDQYL *ZMHPA AMKDT.

BY MIKE SHENK

LABYRINTH

There are two types of answers in this puzzle: Across and Winding. The Across answers consist of two words for each numbered row, each pair entered consecutively, one letter per square. Each pair of Across answers has a total of 12 letters, though the lengths of the individual words vary. The Winding answers snake through the grid, following the labyrinth formed by the heavy bars. These words (numbered for convenience only) are entered in the labyrinth consecutively, beginning in the top left square of the grid, proceeding around to the right, and ending in the first square of the second row. *ANSWER, PAGE 123*

ANSWER, PAGE 123

ACROSS

1 Labyrinth
Laughs gleefully
2 Having being
Confessional confessions
3 Shipbuilding ribs
Trail follower
4 Mixed
The Wise Men

5 Compensation for loss
Frothing at the mouth
6 TV pictures
Actress/singer Bernadette
7 Stinks
Mares-to-be
8 Printed goofs
Calm
9 The hoi polloi
Actor William

10 Set ablaze
Fanatical follower
11 "Woe is me!"
Wall paintings
12 Inventive
It "has a thousand eyes"

WINDING

1 Makes the most of
2 Gave the orders
3 Is in accord
4 *M*A*S*H* props
5 Iran-contra figure Oliver
6 Grasping at straws
7 One with two better halves?

8 Portrait
9 Disencumbers
10 Takes umbrage at
11 Of church studies
12 Closeup of a painting
13 Sandwich shop
14 Thom McAn product
15 Recipient of many blessings?

16 Hoist
17 Browses through a book
18 He'll bet against you
19 Synagogue VIP
20 Throttle
21 More attractive
22 Arab princedom

SIGNIFICANT OTHERS

One day at the Significant Other Dating Service, the pairing coordinator found six new applications—from three men (Janus, Mario, and Julio) and three women (April, Mae, and June)—waiting on her desk. A quick perusal of the applications told her with an awful clarity that the information they had provided was almost entirely astrological. She decided that her best course of action was to match them with each other. To get on top of the situation she phoned an informed contact for an update on the basics, and thereby sorted out the earth signs (Taurus, Virgo, Capricorn), air signs (Gemini, Libra, Aquarius), fire signs (Aries, Leo, Sagittarius), and water signs (Cancer, Scorpio, Pisces). After observing with a vague satisfaction that the six people's sun signs (birth dates) and rising signs (birth times) together encompassed the twelve signs of the zodiac, she saw that she could make three satisfactory, according-to-request, male-female pairings based on sun signs and rising signs alone. She carried through on it pronto, and smoothly coordinated three firm dates exactly as planned.

From the following clues, can you reconstruct the matched-up pairs by full names, sun signs, and rising signs?

ANSWER, PAGE 124

CLUES

1. Mario and Ms. Ramm—both of whose suns are in water signs—were not matched up with each other.
2. The woman with Pisces rising was matched up with Bulley.
3. Of the six applicants, a woman (but not June) was the only one with sun sign and rising sign of the same element (earth, air, fire, or water).
4. Crabbe's Aquarius was paired with another's Libra (both sun or both rising).
5. April—whose application specifically nixed anyone with a prominent Scorpio or Virgo—is herself a combination of an air sign and a fire sign.
6. Fishman was matched up with a sun in Taurus.
7. Julio and Ms. Goatz have rising signs in Aries and Gemini, respectively.
8. The mate who was found for Janus has her sun in Capricorn.
9. Lions does not have Leo rising.

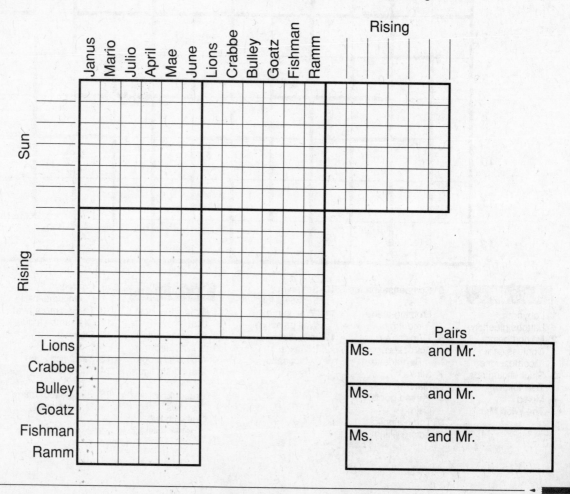

RIGHT ANGLES

The special twist of RightAngles is that each word or phrase, when entered in the puzzle grid, makes one right-angle turn somewhere along its length. It's up to you to determine where each word makes this turn and in what direction.

As a guide, the starting direction of each answer word (*before* the right-angle turn) is indicated by a letter after the clue number: N for north, S for south, and so on. Of additional help is the fact that each letter in the correctly completed grid appears in exactly two words, no more, no less.

For RightAngles #1, the words to be entered in the grid are listed. One answer has been filled in to start you off.

For RightAngles #2, only the definitions of the answer words are given, with the number of letters in each answer in parentheses. *ANSWERS, PAGE 123*

#1—Fill-In

1			2		
	3	4	5		
			6		
			7 L		
			O	8	9
10	11	12	13 G	14 J	A M
15	16		17		18
19	20				

#2—Square Deal

1	2		3		4
		5	6		7
8					9
10				11	12	13
	14				15
					16
		17		18	
19		20	21		

1E BORZOI	**10S** URAL	**1S** Status ___ (3)	**13S** Law specialists (7)
2W AEROBIC	**11W** QUARTO	**2S** Card game for one (9)	**14W** Half a sextet (4)
3W ZOIC	**12N** THOU	**3W** Spicy, as a joke (6)	**15W** Card packs (5)
4S WHELM	**13S** GLARES	**4E** Kind of uncle or treat (5)	**15S** "Scars" on cars (5)
4N WEASEL	**14N** JUMPSHOT	**5N** Made public; ventilated (5)	**16S** Card game for two (3)
5E STIFF-ARM	**15W** RANDY	**6E** Card game for two to four (8)	**17W** Cribbage score marker (3)
6E SPARTAN	**16E** NON	**6S** Card game for one (8)	**17S** Card game for gamblers (5)
7S LOGJAM	**17S** CRANIA	**7S** Worthless horses (4)	**18W** Poke fun at (3)
8N TRAITS	**18S** USE	**8E** *Born Free* lioness (4)	**19E** Tear apart (4)
9N RAFFLES	**18W** UNCLOTHE	**9W** Card game for two to six (7)	**20N** Numbers game for casino
	19N LANDAU	**10E** Word with end or sweet (6)	gamblers (4)
	20N INQUIRY	**10S** Card game for four (6)	**21E** Chief Norse god (4)
		11W Bottled spirit? (5)	
		12N Boy with a motto? (5)	

CROSS-EXAMINATION

ANSWER, PAGE 123

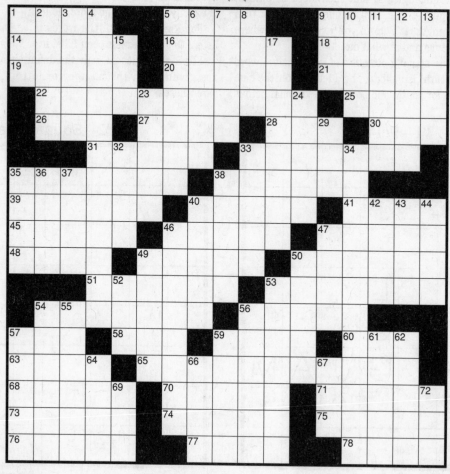

ACROSS

1 LP, e.g.
5 Basis of a deal?
9 German medal
14 Modern fabric
16 Dramatis personae
18 Star
19 Ruth's mother-in-law
20 "___ we all?"
21 Tribal weapon
22 (Self-explanatory)
25 Skin
26 Wellness teaching
27 Vast areas
28 Fraternity character?
30 Mate for Carol (or was it Alice?)
31 Midwest landing site
33 Ill-fated
35 Business
38 Conviction
39 Emblems of St. Anthony
40 Man with a ring
41 "Zounds!"
45 They're most unusual
46 Compelled to go
47 One may finally get the picture
48 Shirt type
49 Black birds
50 Campaign handout
51 Microscopist's view
53 Most sordid
54 Crist and Krantz
56 Board
57 What Boleyn didn't have
58 Words often following "Ode"
59 Hurl
60 "___ ... I Said" (Neil Diamond hit)
63 Field sport
65 This is one
68 Squads
70 Ditch, in a way
71 Met headliner
73 Like some keys
74 Mailroom gadget
75 Baker or Pointer
76 Symbols: It.
77 Digital readouts
78 Old-style romance

DOWN

1 An Everly brother
2 In a huff
3 Delays
4 Be forced to decide
5 Bedtime stories?
6 Pulmonary arteries' kin
7 Hammock rigging
8 Vegas game
9 Scientific suffix
10 He played Batman's Chief O'Hara
11 Acid salt of a type
12 Bordered on
13 Hybridized
15 Diarist Anaïs
17 Yelled "boo!"
23 Despotic leaders
24 Line of sight?
29 Miner's quarry
32 Hastens
33 Battle of the ___
34 Creating beefalo, e.g.
35 On
36 Italian city on the Adriatic
37 Gas, e.g.
38 Italian wine brand
40 Points, in fencing?
42 Pearly portal
43 Murder, She Wrote sheriff
44 Fender bender
46 Brayed
47 Seethe
49 Rugged cycle race
50 African language group
52 Cambridge school
53 They're seeking air
54 Chachi's girl
55 Straightening out, in a way
56 Like Crawford's shoulders
57 Urban eyesores
59 Orange box
61 Kate's mate
62 Tuna concoctions
64 Collar variety
66 Squashed circle
67 Half a Gabor?
69 ___ Lanka
72 Remained

PENCIL POINTERS 7

In this crossword the clues appear in the grid itself. Enter the answers in the direction of the pointers.

ANSWER, PAGE 124

Year of Irangate hearings	"__ soup yet?"	C sharp or B flat	Israel's Abba __	Scrabble piece	Self-centered action	Confine in a zoo		Diner or cafe	Angers	Pesky insect	Religious maverick	"The Georgia Peach"		Soap opera	Verve	Sell	Unit of work	No, to Nikita
Edna Ferber novel						Chili con __						Low-calorie veggie						
Author Calvino						Shed __ (cry)						Sunkist fruit						
Basic belief						*Beau* __						Lash together					Scott Joplin's jazz style	
Lion-hunting trek	"Rapture" singer Baker	Deadly	Open-mouthed in awe	One with regrets					Moose-like deer	Oompah-making horn					Obscure facts	San Giacomo and Dern		Hoed the garden
					Large fancy vase	Fabled snowman Treaties					Sessions run by mediums	Richard Dysart's TV show						
Rundown horse			Young dog					Tom Brokaw's beat		Jefferson Davis's org.			Fury					
Call __ day (quit)			Patio seat	Major or corporal					Siege of Troy story	CBS anchor		Blood fluids	__ as a button					
Gregory Hines's forte									Actress Lupino et al.				Like the Sahara					
Away from the wind				Actress Remick	Like regular highways								Christen					
Film a second time	Actress Sommer	Post office delivery	Category Picnic pests					Rose, as prices										
					Mauna __	Like draft beer	High school student	Region					Asian palm product	Give stars to a movie	Dwelling	More state-of-the-art	Posts, as a letter
Arthur's best knight								Marx's __ *Kapital*				Healthful grains Draft org.					
__ and kin				Dollar bills					Sailor's rum drink		Naval builder						
Born Free lioness				Had lunch				Deserted western city									
Way to get off a highway	Like porno movies	Element added to salt	Swindled	Chicken __ king	Tennis star Agassi						Sown Actress Lauren						
						Jane of workout fame	Sphere Like helium				Scandi-navian		Sounds of hesitation				
Kanga's child			Relieves (of)	File folder parts	Newton filling "Sure!"					Advice writer Landers				Actress Moreno	Examine closely	*St. __'s Fire*	"Children should be __ ..."
Worship									Fish eggs	Entree and dessert							
Kon-__				Daisy Mae's husband						"The" or "an"							
Author Bagnold				Sleeping bags									Not too exciting				
Lairs				Declare					Neighbor of Israel								

PIONEERING PUZZLES

America's best source of puzzles 125 years ago was a rural magazine called the *American Agriculturist*. Founded in 1842, the *Agriculturist* grew into the country's leading farm publication by dispensing practical advice on down-to-earth topics like "Profitable Corn Raising" and "Beet Sugar—Important Experiments."

To help broaden its appeal to farm families, in 1857 the magazine added a monthly column called "New Puzzles to be Answered," an assortment of word games, mathematical problems, rebuses, geometrical puzzles, and other brainteasers both old and new. The column was the pet project of Orange Judd, the publisher of the *Agriculturist*, who, despite all his other duties, edited the feature himself. He once admitted, "I enjoy this department more than all the rest of the paper."

Most of the *Agriculturist*'s puzzles were contributed by readers. Some were already classics when they appeared; others that are now classics appeared there for the first time. The great American puzzlemaker Sam Loyd was one of several puzzlers who borrowed liberally from its pages.

On these two pages are six sample puzzles from the column, all from the 1860s—great puzzles that some of our great-grandparents did. How many can you solve?

ANSWERS, PAGE 124

1. A REMARKABLE BOUQUET

Hidden in the engraving below are profile images of Napoleon I, his wife Maria Louisa, and their son Napoleon II. Can you find them? It is said that when the Bourbons were restored to the French throne, it was forbidden by law to exhibit portraits of the exiled Napoleon or his family. An ingenious young Frenchman devised this method of presenting the likenesses without fear of detection. Thousands of them were readily sold.

2. CHARACTER EVALUATION

Can you properly interpret the letters below to discover a piece of good advice?

Ktt K U U
Khh

P E A Kc E

3. PICTURE POWER

What common proverb is represented by the objects and letters below?

4. LEGAL QUESTION

Can you solve this apparent legal paradox?

Brown and Brooks went out hunting. Brown killed Brooks deliberately but Brown was not guilty of murder.

Why not?

5. FOR SHARP EYES

If you get the right angle on this puzzle, you'll discover both a question and its answer. How?

6. PATH TO FORTUNE

Find your way to fortune by entering at the bottom center of this maze and traveling to the center. As is often true of old mazes, there is more than one correct path—but finding even one may not be so easy.

CRYPTIC CROSSWORD 2

Each clue in a cryptic crossword contains two parts: a definition of the answer and a second description of it through wordplay. Finding the dividing point between parts is the key to solving.

Watch for anagrams, hidden words, charades of two or more smaller words, and other language tricks.

ANSWER, PAGE 124

ACROSS

1 Gets rid of Chinese boats (5)

4 Increases delayed in unusual cases (9)

9 Unknown stranger in gray taking in-depth pictures? (1-6)

10 Token bit of venom in a lecture (7)

11 Exact punishment for Geneva's rioting (6)

12 Makes wagers to take in remarkably fine profits (8)

14 Exotic lout and his converts (10)

15 When every second counts, perform dance (4)

18 Orient animal that starts late (4)

20 Change sun to moon around globe without variation (10)

23 Following an idea, a jerk is tailing those people (8)

24 Sounds like an equal surface (6)

26 Heartless aunt's husband has broken free (7)

27 Plant right half of huge thorn (7)

28 Ranches I dance round, surrounded by bears (9)

29 Group used a car (5)

DOWN

1 Put together *Expo*, just a novel (9)

2 It's most tidy to dine in home (7)

3 Fish straying about . . . (8)

4 . . . therefore monster turned up (4)

5 Against account change (10)

6 Awkwardly move wood (6)

7 Port with more zest (7)

8 Auctions boats in the sound (5)

13 "Counterfeit diamond rings," she warned (10)

16 Low strips rising in distance (9)

17 Almost come upon 20 shillings increase (8)

19 Woman lifted ring up for a fancy finish (7)

21 Perennial bother over inside of sandwich cookie (7)

22 Area around a fancy home (6)

23 How Daffy Duck Pronounced Cease-Fire: The Inside Story (5)

25 Rotates uncovered vases (4)

	1M	2Y	3D	4L	5N	6F	7R		8V	9K	10B	11G	12T	13J	14Q		15A	16U	17O		18C	19M	20S
21I	22B	23P	24W	25F	26A		27S	28D		29O	30L		31N	32H		33T	34P	35K	36B	37M	38F	39R
40S	41E	42V	43J	44Q	45G	46U		47N	48X	49P		50T	51I	52Y		53K	54C	55J	56W	57F	58S	59V
60O	61T		62L		63D	64G	65U	66E	67M		68P	69V	70N	71X	72B	73F	74W	75A		76J	77T	78U
79M		80K	81H	82O	83P	84S		85L	86N		87I	88E	89Y	90J	91U		92D	93R		94F	95B	96S	97I
	98N	99C	100J		101K	102E	103H		104O	105X	106N	107A	108W	109M	110S		111G	112B	113E		114L	115P
116F	117Q	118R	119H	120T	121A		122M	123S	124B		125G	126U		127O	128C	129D	130G	131L	132Q	133M		134X	135Y
136O	137J	138K	139B	140G	141U	142F	143Y		144J	145S	146A		147W	148I	149L		150M	151Q	152B	153D	154P
155X	156F		157S	158G	159V		160T	161U	162P	163R	164L	165E		166C	167B	168V	169M	170F	171K	172X		173H	174J
	175L	176Y	177D	178M		179N	180T	181O	182A	183C	184S		185W	186M	187O	188L						

A. Entice through flattery
121 15 75 107 26 182 146

B. Author of *Billy Bathgate* (3 wds.)
152 22 36 112 10 72 95 139 167 124

C. Sherlock Holmes's bailiwick
183 99 54 18 128 166

D. Last of Stephen King's Richard Bachman books
92 63 3 28 129 177 153

E. Hebrew name for God
165 66 88 113 41 102

F. 1973 Joseph Wambaugh novel (with *The*) (2 wds.)
156 6 73 57 38 116 170 25 94 142

G. Tree-climbing bird that gleans insects from bark
130 64 11 158 140 125 45 111

H. Nicholas Gage book about WW2 activities in Greece
81 119 103 32 173

I. Spiral-shelled marine snail
87 51 21 148 97

J. Newsmaking bus passenger of 1955 (2 wds.)
100 13 174 76 43 144 90 55 137

K. Perceives
9 171 101 53 35 138 80

L. He's likely to pass the bar
188 30 131 4 85 114 62 149 175 164

M. Her first important novel was *The House of Mirth* (2 wds.)
19 109 37 133 122 1 169 79 178
150 186 67

N. Lowest classes of humanity
106 5 47 70 179 31 86 98

O. Study of change in word forms and meanings
17 136 29 181 82 104 60 127 187

P. Early women's gymnastics wear
34 68 23 115 162 154 49 83

Q. Methuselah's "old man"
44 14 117 132 151

R. Russian author of *Dead Souls*
39 163 7 93 118

S. Homes for professorial elephants? (2 wds.)
27 20 96 145 184 157 123 58 84
40 110

T. Propose for candidacy
61 120 160 12 77 33 50 180

U. Unsegmented parasitic worm
141 91 65 16 46 126 78 161

V. Overrun to an unwanted degree
69 59 8 159 42 168

W. Incendiary bomb jelly
56 147 24 108 185 74

X. Ethnic enclave
172 105 71 134 155 48

Y. Riverboat pioneer Henry, founder of a Louisiana city
143 135 2 52 176 89

WAY TO GO!

How well do you follow directions? Every word in the list below is entered in the word search exactly as the word suggests. For example, HORIZONTALLY will be found horizontally in the grid, and IN TWO PIECES will be found, yes, in two pieces. All words appear in straight lines except where the words indicate otherwise (such as SPIRALING). Trust the literal word list and your direction will be clear.

ANSWER, PAGE 125

```
A G W R A C R O S S O N D I T V R E N R
U N D E R A C R O S S I E N O E L I V O
T I E D R A W K C A B W H G I R A N I C
U K L E F T T O R I G H T R W T L E N E
R A D E T F E L G N I D A E H I S Z S H
N M D L L H O L P S L M N O R C H E A T
S I R F I N D D I R A T G O H A A P E D
D R A W T S E W E G R I L K E L A O T N
T H W T I N S G I G N I E E N L P T T U
Y H P I U S C E N T E R E D W Y U O N O
O L U R L R E I W D H I S N L O G T M R
T Y L L A T N O Z I R O H E S O N M U A
L M U A G C D H W H E A U R E A I O L T
W G N Z N P I E S G P Q H T L T O T O R
A N D I I O N A G E I S I S E N G T C I
W H R E S G G A D L A N A T V N D O A G
I R C D I E Z A B C T I G O N W E B N H
A E N R R E M O I O E S R E V E R N I T
S V I A E M N E G D E E H T G N O L A G
```

ACROSS	DESCENDING	LEFT TO RIGHT	UPWARD
ALONG THE EDGE	DIAGONALLY	L-SHAPED	VERTICALLY
AROUND THE CORNER	GOING UP	MAKING A U-TURN	V-SHAPED
ASLANT	HEADING LEFT	MEANDERINGLY	WESTWARD
AT RIGHT	HORIZONTALLY	OBLIQUELY	WINDING
BACKWARD	IN A COLUMN	RISING	WITHOUT END
BOTTOM TO TOP	IN A RIGHT ANGLE	SPIRALING	ZIGZAGGING
CENTERED	IN REVERSE	TURNING	Z-SHAPED
CROOKED	IN TWO PIECES	UNDER "ACROSS"	

Directions appear on page 11.

ANSWER, PAGE 124

DANCE PARTIES

ANSWER, PAGE 124

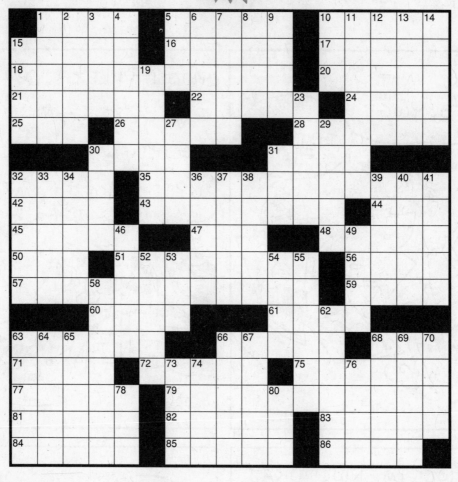

ACROSS

1 Quick study?
5 Take ___ (lose big)
10 Mountaintops
15 Solo
16 Saki's real name
17 Bootblack's offering
18 Dancing Indian?
20 Kunta ___ (*Roots* character)
21 New Orleans university
22 One of Santa's team
24 Got an A on
25 '60s college protest grp.
26 Eagle's claw
28 Cantankerous
30 Miffed
31 Minor argument
32 James of *The Godfather*
35 Dancing singer?
42 "___ Want for Christmas ..."
43 Make a conjecture
44 "The Gold Bug" writer
45 Sales receipts
47 Coloring
48 Coloring
50 Typewriter key
51 Atmosphere
56 Orange skin
57 Dancing president?
59 Summer nuisances
60 ___ the line (obeyed)
61 Drug shipment
63 Arabian Sea port
66 Primitive fishing tool
68 Experimental workshop
71 Whitish gem
72 First name in cosmetics
75 Angry outburst
77 Emulate the Pied Piper
79 Dancing diamond-lover?
81 Actresses Moran and Gray
82 Threepio's fellow droid
83 Motionless
84 Prom, e.g.
85 Charlotte ___ (fancy dessert)
86 Where Cleo barged in?

DOWN

1 Obscure
2 Restaurant freebies
3 "Diana" singer
4 Do on purpose
5 Latin I verb
6 Con game
7 Sultry singer Susan
8 London transport
9 Hydrant attachment
10 Play "20 Questions"
11 Italian wine
12 Chop to bits
13 Walk on stage
14 Dilapidated
15 They may be 1-rm. or 2-rm.
19 San Simeon builder
23 Leon Uris bestseller
27 Jacob's wife
29 Four-star reviews
30 Play the censor
31 "Star Wars," for short
32 Fills film spots
33 Muslim's god
34 Perfect crime part, often
36 "Mixed" items, sometimes
37 *Gaslight* actor Charles
38 "You ___ serious?"
39 Canary Islands owner
40 Cheap dive
41 Tears apart
46 Islands north of Tonga
49 Pitfall
52 "That's what you think!"
53 A following?
54 Relinquish
55 Printing woes
58 Highest of the Alps
62 Source
63 Portended
64 Puccini genre
65 Cheech's last name
66 Ticketholders' entitlement
67 Texas river
68 Record company
69 Idolize
70 Emcee Convy
73 Lasting impression
74 "No ___ Traffic"
76 Sari wearer
78 Mao ___-tung
80 Weeder's need

HEX SIGNS

Each answer in this puzzle is six letters long. These six letters are to be entered into the six hexagons surrounding the appropriate number in the grid, reading clockwise or counterclockwise. The direction and the starting space are for you to determine. Each clue consists of a sentence from which the consecutive letters of the answer have been removed and replaced with a star. The object is to reinstate the missing letters (supplying spacing as needed) to complete a sensible sentence. For example, the answer to #1 is TREMOR, which completes the sentence "The tennis player later felT REMORse for not shaking his opponent's hand." As a bonus hint, each clue also contains a synonym or short definition of the answer (like "shaking" in the example).

ANSWER, PAGE 125

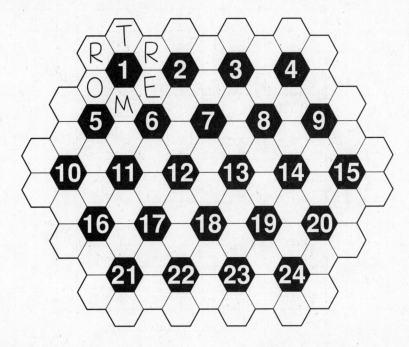

1. The tennis player later fel★se for not shaking his opponent's hand.
2. If you aren't quiet in your apartment, you may not be offered a lea★wal.
3. A pathological li★pecially likely to commit perjury on witness stands.
4. The biology major used faulty gram★ssays about creatures of the sea.
5. In the Far East, it's not unusual to sha★l rooms with total strangers.
6. A group of poli★hwarted the thief, one using his night stick.
7. The teacher and her cl★ered into an agreement on assignments.
8. At the wedding, the groom's cou★tured for the guests to raise their glasses for toasts.
9. The beg★ied stealing any tomatoes from the small vegetable patch.
10. I truly ho★e Janeiro isn't too exciting for a person my age.
11. You can tell that belly dan★mbarrassed by her bright red face.
12. After only one drink, it becomes difficult to con★ope to a hitching post.
13. The singer didn't know whether to sing what he'd originally cho★nother verse of "Lady of Spain."
14. Julian painted his Volksw★rk blue with slate gray trim.
15. Dancers of the t★rely wear wool, since it would get too hot.
16. The whole orchestra was kicked out of the hotel after the woodwind player got to★erous.
17. All but the fi★ather belts may curl up after years of use.
18. Because of his basi★iness, the crook refused to surrender to the authorities.
19. The chief detective on the ca★ucted a thorough investigation from the moment he entered.
20. First-time bowlers may need gui★electing their bowling balls.
21. When asked why he ate so much, the glut★ently indicated he had something in his throat.
22. The archvillain loved to call people names purely fo★ffect.
23. The sharp end of a ra★rtainly could penetrate a dueler's thick coat.
24. The banker asked our print shop to ty★nother copy of his foreign currency exchange rates.

ABOUT FACE

This diagramless is 21 squares wide by 21 squares deep and has left-to-right symmetry. As a hint, the location of the starting square is given on the bottom right corner of page 127.

ANSWER, PAGE 124

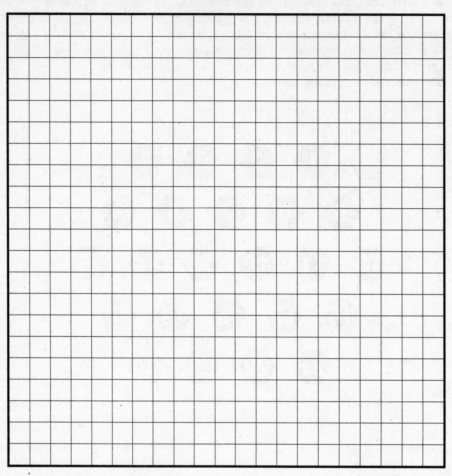

ACROSS

1 Prickly shrub
8 End zones, as in soccer: 2 wds.
10 Meeting points
12 Off the ___ (spontaneously): 4 wds.
14 Trim, as a lawn
15 Bit of paper or chewing gum
16 Ready for payment
18 Letter after "bee"
19 Humorous fellow
22 Tennis tutor
25 ___ Moines, Iowa
27 Like an antique
28 Virtuoso acts
30 Playwright's offering
32 "___ Are My Sunshine"
34 Avant-garde, perhaps: 3 wds.
38 Mexican resort town
39 Book locale
40 TV show
42 Conclusion
43 Asia Minor region
44 All the rage
45 "Act your ___ !"
46 Illegally seize
49 Grand Canyon animal
52 Needlefish
53 French possessive
54 Baseball team
55 Garish
56 ___ generis (unique)
57 Chow down
58 Easily noticed: 3 wds.
64 Flight schedule info.
65 Noisy clamor
67 Cooperative negotiation
68 Car of the 1920s
69 *Dukes of Hazzard* spinoff
71 Saddens
72 Koppel and Kennedy
73 Suffix with sock or buck
75 Greek war god
76 "I won't tell a soul": 4 wds.
86 With much emotion
87 Places to pick up dates?
88 Tie ___ (get drunk): 2 wds.
89 Morning moisture

DOWN

1 Cher's ex Sonny
2 Rabble
3 Permit
4 ___ Loa, Hawaii
5 Pedigree information
6 Telescope component
7 Apiece
8 The "elephant" party
9 Visualize
10 One of a kine?
11 Blue
12 A "little piggy"
13 Failure
14 Noted Florentine family
17 Pooh's donkey friend
18 Like conspirators' meetings
19 Took the gold
20 High school math: Abbr.
21 Grapevine produce?
22 Quickly-built house
23 Author Bradbury
24 House in 29-Down
26 Beginning, figuratively: 2 wds.
27 Citric cooler
28 Prison for a mob traitor?: 2 wds.
29 London restaurant district
30 Sandwich shop
31 Esoteric
33 Some lemons: 2 wds.
35 One-time Bush Chief of Staff
36 Restroom door sign
37 Got back on the carousel
38 Desist's partner
41 Damascus's country
47 Brought to ruin
48 *Superman* star Christopher
50 Arm bones
51 Corner pieces, in chess
59 Sales agent, for short
60 Galley propeller
61 SSW's opposite
62 Meese and McMahon
63 Avenues: Abbr.
66 Standard
68 Clarinet part
70 Oriental beans
72 Three-spot
74 Bullfighting cry
75 100%
77 Common business abbr.
78 Harper Valley org.
79 Missile housing
80 Put right
81 Tennis star Richards
82 Finance, as the arts
83 Ollie's comedy partner
84 Cornfield unit
85 Jolson and Capp

BY BECKY McKIBBEN

DOUBLE CROSS 10

Directions appear on page 15.

ANSWER, PAGE 126

1Q		2H	3F	4N	5C	6P	7E		8J	9R	10S	11T		12G	13H	14K	15D	16R	17P		18Q	19I
20L	21D	22E		23N	24H		25F		26M	27H	28D	29Q		30F	31M	32R	33P	34L	35Q		36A	37G
38K	39Q	40R	41N		42T	43E	44G	45M	46Q	47K	48R	49B	50O		51T	52F	53H	54M		55P	56Q	57E
	58D	59N	60J	61L		62R	63P		64H	65J		66N	67D	68E	69S	70B		71T	72B	73J	74Q	75P
76I	77F		78L	79I	80B	81D	82E		83C	84Q	85R	86D	87N	88I	89J	90C		91A	92C	93O		94R
95P		96L	97D		98D	99E	100A		101B	102L	103Q	104C	105T	106F	107H	108R	109D	110G	111O		112S	113Q
	114S	115D	116R	117N	118I		119T	120G	121S	122J	123M	124C		125R	126D		127K	128B	129M	130I	131N	132O
	133E	134H	135T		136E	137A	138O	139J		140M		141G	142T	143I		144Q	145C	146J	147D	148E		149A
150P	151B	152D		153K	154G	155R		156T	157B	158N	159M		160K	161P		162K	163P		164N	165T	166R	167F
168L		169A	170G	171E	172K	173L	174R	175Q		176F	177I	178M	179E	180O	181C	182D		183E	184O	185J	186M

A. Dog, in baby talk
　36　91　149　169　137　100

B. Canines
　101　70　157　151　49　128　80　72

C. Contradicting
　92　83　124　5　145　104　181　90

D. Reason for a vacation (3 wds.)
　28　152　67　21　182　86　115　98　126
　147　15　109　81　58　97

E. 1974 bestseller on the Manson murders (2 wds.)
　133　57　183　171　43　82　7　148　22
　136　179　99　68

F. Lassitude
　3　106　167　30　25　52　176　77

G. Said with raised voice and fist-pounding
　37　12　44　154　120　110　170　141

H. Japanese admiral portrayed in *Tora! Tora! Tora!*
　13　2　107　27　64　134　24　53

I. Indicator of vitality, in palmistry
　76　88　79　177　19　130　143　118

J. Developing into bone
　73　60　185　122　8　65　146　89　139

K. Puts up with
　14　153　160　162　47　38　172　127

L. Science of classification
　61　78　102　20　34　173　96　168

M. Substance in a futuristic energy chamber
　45　123　159　140　54　31　178　186　129　26

N. The Fourth Estate, traditionally
　131　41　4　158　66　23　164　59　87　117

O. Wild dogs of Australia
　50　180　138　132　184　93　111

P. Equal (hyph.)
　17　150　95　55　163　161　33　63　75　6

Q. Directing, as from behind the scenes
　39　46　103　56　29　144　113　74　18
　175　1　84　35

R. Undisclosed purpose (2 wds.)
　174　16　48　108　166　9　94　116　40
　62　85　125　32　155

S. Certainly (sl.)
　10　112　69　121　114

T. Some heavenly bodies—or circus notables? (2 wds.)
　11　135　165　119　51　42　105　142　156　71

The words that are missing in this mystery story will   puzzle will decipher the story. (**A** = Across, **D** = Down)
solve the crossword puzzle, and vice versa—solving the

ANSWER, PAGE 126

It's funny—**42A** Harbor always **15D** me of my first case, that **13D** day in the last **31A** of 1986 when, on a snowy morning, a distress call reached my office. When the phone rang, I could hardly believe my **43A**: an actual client, telling me that a **27A** had been stolen!

My mind aswirl with visions of riches by the sackful, I roused myself from the **10D** daze, the **25D** torpor (practically a **47D**) in which I'd languished since renting the office from my greedy **26D**, our family slumlord. I grabbed my keys, my coat, and my purse and hopped into my little **36A** (the only thing I'd kept after my **20A** from my husband), and headed out Grove St. to Maple and Oak **12A**, and then to **33A** 80, toward an out-of-town address. The snow was heavy, and the heater in my **36A** wasn't working. What was true in the beginning remains true: Nobody ever **35A** a shamus on a nice day.

As I struggled along at about 20 miles **7D** hour, thinking about the **27A**, I pictured a rich widower or a wealthy **35D** who would gladly **1A** a **51A** young gumshoe like me **42D** of dough to recover the goods. But when I arrived, the building didn't look

29D (2 wds.) swanky nor the grounds especially **9D**, with their unkempt thorny **28D** bushes (though the **44D** yard did **36D** a little pond with a man-made **19A** in it where some ducks, possibly **39A**, were huddled). Inside, in the lobby, a crude sign gave the abbreviated message: "**45D** for rent. Call Jack Lambert, **59A**." Another lawyer slumlord, I noted sourly.

The name on the door of the first-floor **44A** was Delgado, so when a teenaged boy answered my knock, I said, "*Como* **50D** *usted?*" The kid just stared. Maybe with all the snow on my coat, I looked like a wild **3D** of Tibet. Certainly I was shivering like an **6D** sufferer.

"Who's the client here, **1D**?" I asked. (Calling people "**1D**" was, I figured, part of the **8A** private-eye patter I had to learn.) "My **27A** is missing!" answered the kid.

So *he* was my client. I looked him over: a pretty nerdy specimen, I thought, with acne **27D** on his puffy face and a nasal voice probably due to a bad case of **40A**.

"Just what valuables," I asked him, "did this **27A** of yours contain?"

"Well," he said, "there's a

42A inside that's very **8D**."

I didn't mean to be **16A**, but I felt my eyebrow **34A**. Why would this kid have a **42A**? And why was it **8D**?

"Where did you last see it?" I asked.

He pointed to a door.

"**58A** here," I said.

"Looking through my **55A**," said the kid, "will be rough."

His **55A**? What kind of a **56A** was he trying to pull? Was this kid a kidder, a mere **39D**? I had to wonder. But I was so **14A** to start my **4D** that I stepped into his bedroom. What I confronted was a scene of typical adolescent disarray, certainly not bad enough to bury anyone in. I spied heaps of clothes, the gear of an **2D** sports nut (including a baseball **49D** with the price **60A** still attached), a **25A** of records (mostly by rock **32A**, though in addition to Van Halen and **38D** Jett I did see **57A** James and **37A** Torme, so maybe the **38A** kid wasn't a completely twerpy lowbrow), plus some scattered foodstuffs (old pizza slices, a bottle of A&W **46D** **11D** with some insect, probably a **18D**, crawling **41D**)—but not the slightest **24A** of the **27A**.

Just then the kid gave a cry, and I darted into the hallway in

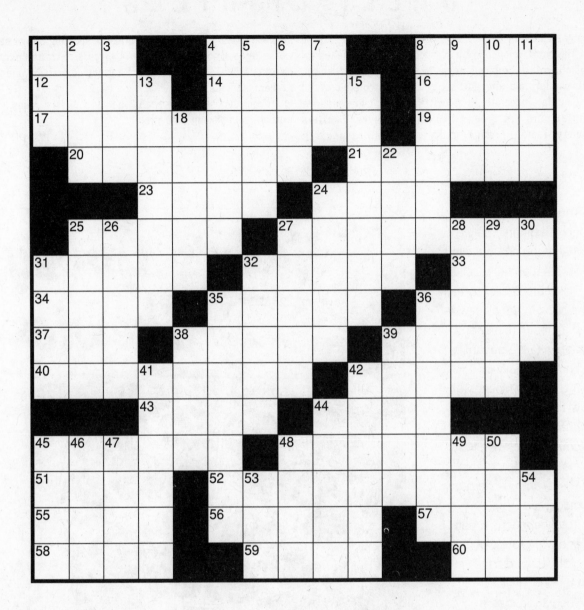

time to see a woman standing there. She looked prim, the sort of lady you'd expect to find at church and **53D** meetings at school, yet she was holding, unfolded, a sample of periodical **17A** not usually associated with her type.

"**31D**," the boy was whining, his face in a sullen **48D**, "how could you rake that from my **55A**?"

What was going on? *"That's* no **27A**!" I cried, a bit stupidly.

"No, I'm sorry," said the boy's smiling **21A**, "but you see, in this family, we tend to **5D** our **32D**."

5D 32D? What did the class **12A** have to do with anything? Then it hit me. **23A** time the kid and his **21A** spoke, they'd uttered a **52A**! (I **48A** you know that this involves a **4A** of sounds.)

So it all made sense, as I gazed at the periodical **17A**, the **54D** with the telltale **43A** on the **44D**.

Case solved, then. And I'll tell you, no matter how cryptically **45A** any case **30D** (and I've had some obscure **22D** over the years), none matches that first caper for quirky humor. I didn't even mind that they couldn't **1A** me. As I said to them in parting, "**37A**, **24D** isn't everything."

BY ROBERT E. NELSON

SWEET EIGHTEEN

A company located in Sweet Home, Oregon, has begun making candies. The outfit, known as Huey's Gooey Chewies, makes six types of chocolate-covered nuts (peanut, pecan, cashew, hazelnut, walnut, and almond), six types of chocolate-covered creams (vanilla, chocolate, strawberry, mocha, marshmallow, and maple), and six types of chocolate-covered jellies (strawberry, lemon, orange, mint, apple, and raspberry).

An advertising poster has been made, showing one of each type of Huey's Gooey Chewies in a circular arrangement of six sections. Within each section is a group comprising one nut, one cream, and one jelly.

From the clues below, can you locate all 18 candies, group by group, going around the circle?

ANSWER, PAGE 126

1. The almond's group comes directly between that of the orange jelly and that of the hazelnut.

2. The marshmallow cream is two groups clockwise from the mint jelly and opposite the pecan.

3. The apple jelly is two groups clockwise from the cashew, and two groups counterclockwise from the strawberry cream.

4. The peanut is one group clockwise from the mocha cream, and two groups counterclockwise from the raspberry jelly.

5. The vanilla cream is opposite the strawberry jelly.

6. The lemon jelly is two groups clockwise from the maple cream, and two groups counterclockwise from the hazelnut.

7. The two strawberry candies are in different groups.

Huey's Gooey Chewies are yummy to the tummy!

BY MAREK PENSZKO

POLISH YOUR WITS

A good brainteaser, says Polish puzzle whiz Marek Penszko, has "some original, new, interesting, and simple idea." Herewith three examples with which to tickle your gray matter.

ANSWERS, PAGE 126

1. A SWITCH IN TIME SAVES NINE

The nine numbered cards below form an "almost magic" square. It would be completely magic if the sum of the numbers in every row, column, and diagonal were the same. (Right now the diagonal from the upper left to the lower right is the only line that doesn't match.) Can you change the places of exactly three cards to form a completely magic square?

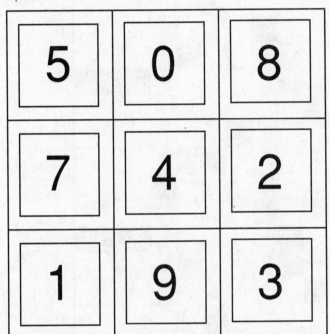

2. DON'T WORRY, BE HAPPY

This addition includes only three different numbers, which are pictured as three kinds of faces. But four of these faces are shy and have turned away. Can you decipher the sum?

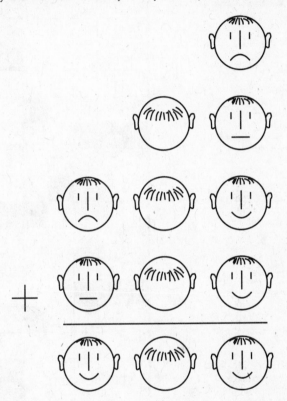

3. SQUARING UP

Change the position of two tetromino blocks so that the inner territory is still enclosed and now contains 15 squares.

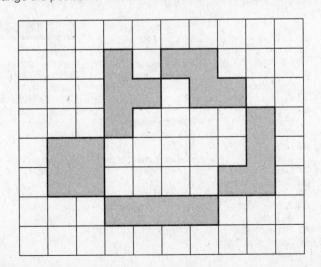 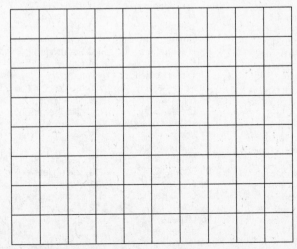

BY MIKE SHENK

BOXING MATCH

In addition to the usual Across and Down clues, this puzzle has
seven Box clues. Each of these leads to an eight-letter answer
that can be found within the completed grid in the form of a
box surrounding a single extra letter and reading either
clockwise or counterclockwise. For example, in the grid section
at right, the word SPECIMEN can be found starting with the

s and reading counterclockwise. When
you've found the seven Box answers in the
grid, take the letters they surround (like the
o in the example), in the order of the Box
clues, to identify the person to whom this
puzzle is dedicated.   *ANSWER, PAGE 126*

I	C	E
M	O	P
E	N	S

ACROSS

1 Italian cheese town
6 Where runs are scored
11 At ___ (with some drawbacks)
16 *Let's Make ___*
17 *Home Folks* poet
18 Oahu veranda
19 Vanzetti's cohort
20 Daffy
21 Sell for
22 Hunters, anglers, etc.
24 Class member
26 Sicilian spouter
27 "... man ___ mouse?"
28 Pack quantity
29 "Able was ___ ...."
30 Highfalutin home
32 Ready for future use
34 Cosmetics expert Rubinstein and others
37 Doggerel creator
41 1960 movie bio
42 Tricky stratagem
44 What *lento* signifies
45 "Book 'em, ___" (*Hawaii Five-O* line)
47 Founts of wisdom
49 Prerequisite
50 Channel swimmer Gertrude
53 Like some numbers or killers
56 Stocking-hanging time
57 York and Pepper
59 Fearful fellow
61 Daisy's lookalike
62 Flipper's call
63 "Jeopardy" singer Greg
66 Opposing verdict
67 Decline
68 "Spirit of 1776" instrument
72 Beset by difficulty
74 Shrimp, crabs, lobsters, etc.
76 Chef's sample
77 Old anesthetic
79 Actor Jeremy
80 Kiki's "Don't Go Breaking My Heart" co-singer
81 Lover
82 Arthur Murray's forte
83 Feeds the piggies
84 Cartography dots
85 Lisper's challenges

DOWN

1 Just not done any more
2 Rewrite for the screen
3 Scout's job
4 Craftsy wall hanging
5 Oodles
6 Path flowers?
7 Like the graph y = mx + b
8 Senator Cranston
9 Decimal base
10 Seeing level
11 Provençal morning song
12 Misbehaves childishly
13 Cat-___-tails
14 Possessing more marbles?
15 *León*'s kin
23 Sub tracker
25 Turnoffs?
28 OK fellow?
31 Grasshopper's pal in fable
33 Taciturn Prez
34 Home of the dead
35 Sidestep
36 Highway painter
37 Capitol gofers
38 Casual material
39 *École* attender
40 Painter Albert Pinkham
46 Set of pipes, of a sort
48 Mutton chops, e.g.
51 ___ *Misérables*
52 "... could ___ fat"
54 Lawrence's followers
55 Blazed the trail
58 Most fastidious
60 To the extent that
62 Amid the clauses of this contract
63 High flyers
64 Completely
65 Must
69 Computer screen symbols
70 What he buys is hot stuff
71 Moves gradually
73 Writes
74 Wad of Skoal
75 Surfer's concern
78 Brace

BOXES

A Italian noblewoman
B Equinox's counterpart
C Instruments also called "sweet potatoes"
D Sing to one's sweetie
E "Sawbucks"
F Capital of South Australia
G Deep and full, as a voice

BY TRIP PAYNE

CHANGE PLACES

There are two Across clues for each row in this cryptic crossword puzzle. Before you can enter these words into the grid, one letter from the first word must change places with a letter from the second word in order to form two *new* words. (For example, if the clues for one row lead to the words STOOP and RILED, you might enter STROP and OILED into the grid.)

The Down clues, which are normal, will help you determine which letters are interchanged. When you've completed the grid, copy each changed letter into the extreme left or right column (whichever it's closer to in the grid); these columns will contain appropriate phrases. Clue answers include six proper names.

ANSWER, PAGE 127

ACROSS

1 Folds pastel slips (6)
5 Outshines former third-class trains (6)
9 Theater awards Boise trips (5)
10 Fungus shape (4)
11 Thicken back and front of sinewy limbs (4)
12 More theatrical disguise is great (7)
13 Lumberman's beer mentioned (6)
14 One entering southeast sound (4)
16 Final in biology soon to be annual (6)
18 Brood over tiny hole (4)
20 Rattle bundle containing bit of ammo (6)
23 Regret having love for wolf (4)
27 *Times* article intrudes on hospital rooms (4)
28 Correspondent is more accurate sounding (6)
29 Poorest diet seen in a stew (8)
30 Hauls tippler back, consuming fifth of firewater (4)
31 Discusses hunt beginning to end? (5)
32 Macbeth and others hasten to change (6)

DOWN

1 Said to take money for small room (4)
2 Loyal subject, for example, caught in falsehood (5)
3 Takes in a bishop with small eyes (7)
4 Rent, to nurse (4)
5 Recite Old Testament book in compound (5)
6 Alternately, spring is for swine (4)
7 Composer's large broadcast (5)
8 Orgy, per se, is kinky (5)
10 Biblical woman's reforming army (4)
13 Victory wreath's strange allure (6)
15 Judge never keeps inheritance from ancestors? (4)
17 Urge confining me to Mideast country (5)
19 Circle part of news item (4)
20 Unsurpassed to be a holy man (4)
21 Live on a terrain (4)
22 *Daily Planet* reporter is after liberal *Globe* (4)
24 Curse at, interrupting sound of surprise (4)
25 Returning memo and finishing school (4)
26 Reportedly makes coffeepots (4)

REBUS RIOT

Whoever invented spelling may have been on the wrong track. After all, why spell a word with seven letters when you can do it with four? And who says you always have to line up the letters from left to right? Arranging them in other ways can often yield interesting results.

To solve this word search puzzle, first answer as many of the 36 rebuses below as you can. Each answer is a word that is literally described by the groupings and relative positions of the letters shown. For instance, the first rebus represents the word ABANDON (AB and ON), while the second is ABYSMALLY (A by small Y).

All 36 words (including ABANDON and ABYSMALLY) can be found in the word search grid, each reading in a straight line vertically, horizontally, or diagonally. Work back and forth between the grid and rebuses to get the answer words that you miss the first time through. As a solving aid, the 36 rebuses are given in alphabetical order of their answers, and the number of letters in each is shown in parentheses.

WORD LIST, PAGE 125

ANSWER, PAGE 127

```
E W E F I L F L A H S I R E V O P M I S
N B Y O R D S L M P I N O C H L E A Y H
O Y T L N O D N A B A S O N N E T P B O
D G H E L A N C I S A T U R A T E A N W
N O G T F A I E P N H B E L I T T L E D
O N U R U D M R D H I B O R S M E C A O
C E A N N O I S T N E R A P D N A R G W
L S N A S N T N Y R E V O C S I D E O N
O S H F T O I N C B O T M M K U N D O E
V O T E N R I C I C A M P G R O U N D T
E R D E Y S S U B R E D N U L B E U E W
R C A B L T I O E N P B U T K H T H D O
L A A H E P Y C O U P O N S T C A T I R
E L L A H T I W E R E H W R R E O F O K
A U T F A R C R E V O H A N W R E L V S
F E R U T X I M T S P P Y S R E T F A R
```

AB ON (7)	CL LEAF (10)	GR + P ≠ S (12)	L̸E (8)	OCH(P)LE (8)	S NET (6)
Ay (9)			K C O L (6)	U(PR)T (8)	
A̶ (7)	C D E (7)	LI (4-4)		SR (7)	S (8)
BEd (9)		HI S (9)	RUTE (7)	SST E (9)	CLAP TH (11)
BUSS BL (11)	CO S (7)	H CRAFT (10)	0Y (7)	SURE (8)	TRICER S (11)
GS A (7)	D = C/Y (9)	IMP ISH (10)	NE RK RK (8)	S H O W (8)	TTT (7)
C M G P (10)	HSALF (9)	T(LAR)H (9)	PAR ON (9; proper name)		WAL (11)

ONE, TWO, THREE

Solve this puzzle as you would a regular crossword *except* that each space may hold one, two, or three letters. The number of letters in a space is for you to determine from logic and the crossing of words. The answer to 1-Across, F-AL-CON, has been filled in as an example.

ANSWER, PAGE 127

ACROSS

1 *The Maltese* ___
4 Item under the hood
8 Photog's devices
12 McDonald's symbol
13 Forms into grain-sized pieces
14 Pre-plumbing "bathrooms"
15 Sidewalk stuff
16 Spy: 2 wds.
17 Rims on metal wheels
18 Sorority
20 In front of the audience
22 Story-telling Uncle
24 Detention in one's own residence: 2 wds.
28 Whirls
31 Publisher's protection
34 Yours, in the Bible
35 Bakery units
36 Healthful orange juice ingredient: 2 wds.
37 Unfair treatment: 2 wds.
38 What % means
39 Finland's neighbor
40 Stoolies
41 Steno's writing
43 Shell-selling site
45 Metal fasteners
48 Cadet's school: 2 wds.
52 The First State
55 Painted new stripes on the highway
57 Impassive one
58 Commence
59 Harmonizes
60 Express gratitude to
61 Flower parts
62 Popular Beatles song
63 Pittsburgh gridder

DOWN

1 Broad comedies
2 Seeker of lead-to-gold conversions
3 He gives agreement
4 Telegrapher's "language": 2 wds.
5 Grow weary
6 Stop sign, for one
7 Takes offense at
8 Disguises for concealment
9 Patriot Allen
10 Cheek reddener
11 Appraise
19 Stable residents
21 Notion
23 Soviet capitalist?
25 Robin's snack
26 North Pole team
27 Real bargains
28 Skiing sites
29 Make very thirsty
30 Patent seeker
32 Giza attraction
33 Enrage
37 Amazon oxygen producer: 2 wds.
39 Graceful entry into the pool: 2 wds.
42 Gives a warning to
44 Lent's start: 2 wds.
46 Pact
47 Blackboards
49 Right away
50 Chant
51 Rib-___ (amusing story)
52 Sandwich shops
53 Bryant or Gillette
54 The early '40s, e.g.
56 Neither masculine nor feminine

105

BY MIKE SHENK

ABRIDGED DICTIONARY

Each rectangle on these pages is an excerpt from *Webster's Ninth New Collegiate Dictionary*. As you can see, the excerpts have been rather severely abridged, so much so that it may be difficult to tell from where in the dictionary they've been taken. For how many of the pieces can you identify the words being defined or illustrated? (Consider your answer correct if you can identify any one of the dictionary entries in the excerpt.) Look for helpful bits of pronunciations, etymologies, and illustrations to make your best guesses.

ANSWERS, PAGE 127

1.

strong sexual desir
ELECTRIC CHAIR
xiety
) 1 : a fast freig
shot *adj*
AL SPRING: *esp* : a

Afrik] (1677) 1 :
akin to both the
tentot people
. wooden tub of h

e in intensity, pace
eginning of Febru
lier

involving actual f

ssing predicament

954) : to start (as
n
OE *hund;* akin to
: DOG b : a dog c
ge drooping ears a
2 : a mean or des
ks or collects some
sue with or as if w
ssing 〈~*ed* from off

2.

1 pseudopo-
ucleus, *3* con-
acuole, *4* food
acuole

a plant part
s a substitute

. ME, fr. OE
ge- (associa-
ongst fr. ME
12c) 1 : in
y or associa-
egate of 〈dis-
iest ~ poets〉
: in shares to
rocal acts of
〈made a for-

s [Sp, fr. *a* to
ry sherry
being neither
which moral
. Thompson〉
outside or be-

3.

n] *syn* see PRECEDING
dj (1600) : PREVIOUS. PAST
onclusion that has preceded argu-
le result : CERTAINTY 〈the victory

n (1695) 1 : the part of a scene or
d in front of the spectator 2 : a

rior part of the alimentary canal of
to the pharynx, esophagus, stom-
intestine

rchaic
: the
er 3
rac-
such

given
n the
ction
ennis

4.

-, *rex* ki
NTY 〈und
fluence o
2 : the

ower : RU
ttle gover
2 : to exe
nant or p

evolution
ts] (1801
itted by

E *imbur*
+ ML
someone
ayment
syn see PA
or-smənt

retina, fr.
stened to
ed in pl.
e proceed
~s of go
gave full

5.

n fire : BLA
ance, or wa
SSIONATE 〈~

es
la-
nc
ds
gs
ill
nt
ge
ng

6)
gh

6.

feast that commemc
variations of date du
he paschal full moon

DATES

YEAR	ASH WEDNESDAY	
1993	Feb	24
1994	Feb	16
1995	Mar	1
1996	Feb	21
1997	Feb	12
1998	Feb	25
1999	Feb	17
2000	Mar	8
2001	Feb	28
2002	Feb	13

dyed bright colors and

white cultivated lilies

7.

rther to the left

her to the right

r fl as ligatures æ or fl

en alignment

own] (13c) 1 a : referring
one : OWN c : appointed for
sented heraldically in natural
a species or individual : PECU
4 : very good : EXCELLENT
: strictly limited to a specified
: strictly accurate : CORRECT
: strictly decorous : GENTEEL
appropriateness : FIT 9 : bei

8.

n\ *adj* (1729)   **1** : worn or impaired by
: AGE-OLD, ANCIENT ⟨~ procedures⟩   **b**
e⟩

hical region within which the same stan-

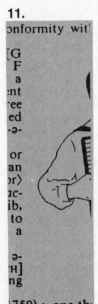

terminous United States: *A* Pacific

9.

126.9045   hairless four
192.22   muscular tru
55.847   male into lar
83.80   forms and va
138.9055   (*Loxodonta*
             b : a relative
207.2   southeastern
6.941   : an animal
174.967
24.305
54.9380

200.59
95.94
144.24
20.179
237.0482
58.69
92.9064
14.0067

190.2
15.9994

10.

the heavens us
of all the princ
line, and is div
logical purpose
senting the sign
~ of feasts an
zə-\ *adj*

	S
NUMBER	
1	An
2	Ta
3	Gc
4	Ca
5	Le
6	Vi
7	Li
8	Sc

11.

onformity wit!

[G
F
a
ent
ree
ed
-ə-

or
an
or)
ac-
ib,
to
a

ə-
H]
ng

(1759) : one tha

haic : RECKON
ries to cover t
erson or conce
d and the resu
ct   **b** : a stat
tisfactory ~
⟨on that ~ I
viding for regu
e credit) and i

12.

) : an offensive football halfback
en an offensive end and tackle
c toy racing automobile that ha
ve for guidance and metal strips
city and that is remotely controll
at
hs *with* ths
w] (12c)   **1**
n or labor
apathy and
~⟩   **2** : any
oreal eden-
it tropical
l America,

13.

68 Ger.
e-sided
a rect-
rotating
degrees,

754)   **1**
ob as a
ə-,krat\
k\ *adj*
a mem-

gonquian origin
t leather heelless
oot and over the
aped piece lying
on the forepart

14.

) : marked by a
syn see FAST —

fast and the sur-
but sing. or pl. in

ement of the eyes

dapted for firing
eliness, or sharp-

or state of being

as by

night

apere

15.

nning : continued rapid
the act of migrating or
e of fish that migrate or
⟨a mile ~⟩   **e** : a score
late safely   **f** : strength
distance made on a run-
⟩   **2 a** *chiefly Midland*
urse of a certain opera-
p in sugar maples⟩   **3 a**
from where it begins to
ection in which a vein of
cleavage : GRAIN ⟨the ~
l distance covered by a
om the wall plate to the
or direction   **4** : a con-
ilar sort: as   **a** : a rapid

Y |
f |

P |
W |

B   M
b   e

RIDDLE-DE-DEE

The letters in the shaded squares, read from top to bottom, will spell the answer to the question at 20- and 86-Across.

ANSWER, PAGE 126

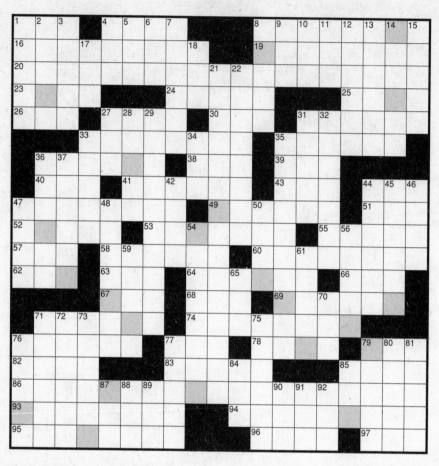

ACROSS

1 "How ___ love thee?"
4 Largest of the seven
8 Potassium ___ (K_2CrO_4)
16 Toast times
19 Nokomis's grandson
20 First half of a riddle
23 Posted
24 D'Artagnan pal
25 Office part-timer
26 Work unit
27 Humorist Wilson
30 Rat-race routine
31 Nixon's sextet
33 Fire insurance?
35 Notifies
36 Six-shooter
38 Veneration
39 Of roses, e.g.
40 Letter abbr.
41 Glassy
43 Boxer's thrust
44 Sternward
47 Chip-dip pepper
49 Mother earth
51 As well
52 Cousin to the giraffe
53 No diehard, he
55 Oak progeny
57 A major, for example
58 Summer holiday, with "the"
60 Georgia college town
62 Mr., and Mr. Meese
63 Calendar abbr.
64 Queen of witches, in *Macbeth*
66 Churchillean sign
67 Vegas opener?
68 ___ glance
69 Be firm
71 Emulate an iceman?
74 Klinger or Agarn
76 Video game parlor
77 Shooting marble
78 Once more
79 Rows 6-8
82 Ten: Prefix
83 Bad guys
85 Hydrox competitor
86 Second half of the riddle
93 Wire
94 Make speechless
95 True copies, in law
96 Carry on
97 "___ Jude"

DOWN

1 Look for water
2 Yellowish pigment
3 Hockey infraction
4 Vesuvius souvenir?
5 General address?
6 Poker marker
7 Tomes of the times
8 Treasure holder
9 Casual greetings
10 Rarer than rare?
11 WW2 agcy.
12 Synagogue reciter
13 Certify
14 Signatures
15 O.K. Corral faction
17 Exploit
18 Plane at JFK
21 Give up
22 Purrfect pet?
27 D.C. hrs.
28 Superior to
29 Give up
31 Fair forecast
32 Himalayan bruin
33 Tin Pan Alley org.
34 One for the road
35 Giving up
36 Wan
37 Dental additions
42 Do Europe
44 Shows he's sorry
45 Exhibit amnesia
46 Muscular fitness
47 Laugh getter
48 Talked nonsense
50 Town near the Gulf of Honduras
54 Some upstate New Yorkers
56 Trivial objection
59 Filibuster
61 Sort
65 Jalopy
70 Magician's prop
71 Flapjacks *français*
72 The supernatural
73 Injurer
75 COD demand?
76 TV oldie, ___ *With Judy*
77 Cowboys and Indians
79 Rabies indication
80 "Three wishes" granter
81 Obviously contrived
84 Opera fans' mecca
85 East End, to a native?
87 Better wine
88 "... ___ mouse?"
89 Stoolie
90 Genetic stuff
91 Urge
92 Cohort of Bea, Betty, and Estelle

DOUBLE CROSS 11

Directions appear on page 15.

ANSWER, PAGE 128

1X	2G		3L	4M	5Y	6B	7K		8N	9S	10A		11C	12H	13J		14Y	15T		16R	17N	18F	19W
20Y		21F	22D	23Q	24B	25L		26Y	27O	28M	29U	30W	31P		32E	33I	34J	35V		36Y	37C		38G
39S	40A	41W	42X		43F	44S		45D	46N	47R	48W	49K		50L	51J	52O	53A		54G	55Q	56T		57R
58L	59I	60P		61N	62B	63M		64B	65V	66W	67L		68N	69S	70D	71P	72O	73Y		74C	75B	76F	77X
	78T	79Y	80U	81V	82E	83L	84Q	85D	86W		87G	88H	89J	90A	91B		92F	93M	94P		95Y	96E	
97I	98T	99S	100K	101J	102W	103D	104B	105L		106T		107C	108X	109G	110N		111T	112P	113Y	114O	115G	116S	117J
118Q		119V	120H	121C	122P	123M		124A	125L	126B	127G	128D	129O	130Y		131T	132K	133B		134L	135V	136W	137N
138Y	139M		140R	141F	142D		143L	144P		145U	146G	147Y	148I	149L		150Y	151W	152F	153C		154L	155I	156A
157E	158Y	159J		160P	161F		162B	163G	164D	165Y	166R	167O	168I	169C	170T		171L		172W	173N	174L	175A	176Y
177V	178H		179P	180S	181C	182Y	183A	184R		185D		186X	187O	188K	189T	190M	191F		192B	193U	194N	195J	196L

A. Recurring
90 183 156 40 10 124 175 53

B. "___ is the great bawd" (*Poor Richard's Almanac*)
62 162 126 75 24 91 133 104 6 192 64

C. 2240 pounds (2 wds.)
107 74 181 153 11 169 121 37

D. Calling forth
142 70 164 128 185 45 103 22 85

E. Split
32 157 82 96

F. Cathode-ray tube used in TV sets
18 43 161 21 191 92 76 152 141

G. Secondary
38 146 115 127 2 87 109 163 54

H. Strap fastener
120 12 178 88

I. Vague thought
59 155 97 168 33 148

J. Science or art of making timepieces
51 117 195 89 101 34 159 13

K. Alternative version, in music
132 188 49 100 7

L. 1778 tragedy in NE Pennsylvania (2 wds.)
50 25 143 154 83 174 105 3 171 125 196 58 134 67 149

M. *Mary Poppins* author
139 190 93 28 4 63 123

N. More or less of an intention (3 wds.)
46 194 68 61 17 8 173 137 110

O. Kinship on the mother's side
114 167 52 129 27 187 72

P. Ad-libbing (2 wds.)
122 71 94 31 160 144 179 112 60

Q. God of love
23 118 55 84

R. Teeming
47 140 57 166 184 16

S. Dilly-dallier
116 99 69 44 180 9 39

T. Made to withstand great strain (hyph.)
98 189 106 15 170 111 56 78 131

U. Old Greek region, home of Olympia
193 80 29 145

V. Having branches
177 135 35 65 119 81

W. Aerodynamics test site (2 wds.)
172 151 41 86 48 66 136 30 19 102

X. Cottonwood
1 186 42 77 108

Y. "Misery acquaints a man with ___" (*The Tempest*; 2 wds.)
130 14 113 36 158 73 147 95 79 5 165 176 150 26 138 182 20

SCHEDULE SCRAMBLE

The new secretary arrived at 8:30 on his first day to find himself faced with the task of assembling a schedule of meetings from the few rough notes left on his desk by his predecessor:

1. Ms. Golding should come before the woman from Sherman's does.
2. The meeting with Quay's should last an hour, but should be shorter than the meeting with Ms. Bunyan in the afternoon.
3. The longest meeting should last an hour longer than the one with Mr. Eliot immediately before it.
4. The meeting with the man from Underwood's should end the day nicely.
5. Make sure the person from Polk's, not Ms. Hardy, comes before the meeting with Reed's.

6. Tell the boss not to mention Chaucer to Fielding—they were recently divorced.
7. The boss likes to take an hour-long lunch starting at 12:30 and leave the office at 6:00.
8. All the meetings take place here, except the morning meeting at Washington's—that's a 15-minute cab ride from here.
9. The meeting with Dickens should take place two hours before the meeting with the person from Vare's.
10. Have a nice day!

In the half-hour before his new boss arrived, the secretary managed to sort out the schedule. Only two meetings were scheduled to last the same amount of time, one in the morning, the other in the afternoon. The duration of each meeting was approximate to the nearest quarter-hour.

Fortunately, everything went according to plan. The woman from Taft's, not Ms. Bunyan, was the only person to arrive at 15 minutes before the hour. No one arrived at 15 minutes past the hour.

The shortest meeting was in the morning, and the longest meeting of the morning began at 10:00. The man from Underwood's was not Mr. Arnold. Four men and four women attended the meetings. No two people with alphabetically adjacent initials attended meetings before or after each other.

Can you draw up the day's schedule, giving the time of each meeting, who attended it, and what company each person represented? *ANSWER, PAGE 128*

	MEETING WITH:	FROM:
9:00		
15		
30		
45		
10:00		
15		
30		
45		
11:00		
15		
30		
45		
12:00		
15		
30		
45		
1:00		
15		

	MEETING WITH:	FROM:
1:30		
45		
2:00		
15		
30		
45		
3:00		
15		
30		
45		
4:00		
15		
30		
45		
5:00		
15		
30		
45		

MARCHING BANDS

The words in this puzzle march around the grid in two ways. In one formation ("Rows"), words march across—two words for each numbered line, reading consecutively from left to right. The dividing point between these answers is for you to determine, except in row 7, where the words are separated by a black square. In the second formation ("Bands"), words march around each of the six shaded and unshaded bands, starting at the lettered squares (A, B, C, D, E, and F) and proceeding in a clockwise direction, one word after another. For example, Band "A," when filled, will contain seven consecutive words (a through g) starting in square "A" and reading around the perimeter of the grid. Band "B" will contain a series of six words (a through f) starting in square "B." Again, the dividing point between these answers is for you to determine. All clues are given in order. When the puzzle is completed, each square in the grid will have been used once in a Row word and once in a Band word.

ANSWER, PAGE 127

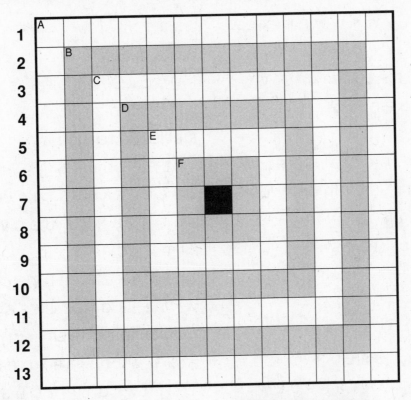

ROWS

1a Groups pursuing desperadoes
b Got to first base
2a Slopped-over amount
b Washer cycle
3a Store driveway sign
b Cupid, for one
4a Wide-screen movie process
b "Purple" bird
5a Noted lamp owner
b Cave
6a Thick soups
b Car frame

7a Infamous fly
b Unfold
8a Time-filling entertainment
b Long, long time, old-style
9a Strainers
b "Oh, no!"
10a Dentist's deadener
b Debatable
11a Like much modern art
b Show of skits
12a Logging chute
b Pass
13a Enchilada's cousin
b Cur

BANDS

Aa Having
b Alpine garb
c Pittsburgh player
d Fantasy creature
e Tibetan VIP
f Planes, trains, cars, etc.
g Acts the expectant father
Ba Vandal, perhaps
b Like frogs and chameleons
c Longtime CBS head William
d Leather piercer
e Timber wolf
f Pancreatic output

Ca ___ Haute, Indiana
b Starts a new paragraph
c Summer sign
d Plain to see
e Supermarket vehicles
f Old soldier
Da Historic time
b The Godfather, e.g.
c Area south of the Caucasus
d Desirable
Ea Bell sound
b Wild talker
c Sounds of surprise
d Irish tongue
Fa Slate

ANSWERS, PAGE 128

1. KEEP SMILING

B D R J   P M H R K   D V B   Q V
G R Q P L J   M Q L Y Y   T W W R G   X L W
L J   Z P Q Q X R ,   Y X L W   N V X V J R X
M T U U R M Q M   R F Q G P   K P Z   V Y
S T M Q P N D R   B P F .

2. BEAT IT!

Y J V K W Q X Z   C U   C W B   H U F X G
U R   N U F V   U M X   G V F Y Y B V   Q H
U D   F X C Q P   N U F   C V N   R U V
B Y T P U N Y B X C   M Q C W   J
H N Y T W U X N .

3. HAIR APPARENT

* B R O W   * P H O T A R   C R Y
Y D R G J .   C M R J   J R L D R V
C H N B O   G T Y F   M N Y S R V O B W
C G R J M   S W   Y K K F T V P   M K G
M T O O K V   R Y Y K J Y ?

4. PLEASANT DREAMS

A N P R V M B ,   Q N S T A R V M B
N S N X W R B N B   T W A   T B
B V F V X R H R W .   R C B V J C R T W B
X N Y L   V C   W X L F A V K X T J B
E R A G   E T X J   J R Y O .

5. BLOCKED SHOT

X Z Y J Z K L   H Z M P N C W D T N W
J S D T N W ,   M V J W C V   F N X X
C N W Q   F V K   V L V Z K D P
P V G Z K L   H U S P S   S X
W R T N Z D Z P W   S Q V Y Z D T N W .

6. BUILDING TENSION

* G L B F V C L Y Z
Y C B P L F K B F N C K ' U
B N C H L B N K J   U B C V H H D V C T ,
X L Z X K C R C K Y J
V C Z Y S K Z F Y F L V Z   X L G K
M Y L Z F K C U   Z L X P F S Y C K U .

7. LANGUAGE BARRIER

* Y X W V U T S   T R X Q P O
N Y M N V Y O Y T   Y O D S P X W Y
T Q J I Y X Q   T Q M J W W V U X W
H U Q S   U M M Y W J V P M   G Y M F T ,
U I U K E P Q D   Y O N M Y T T U K X T .

8. I AM THE GREATEST!

D P C R D M Q X P K   S X S R J Q T R N J B ,
V B J M Q   V B T H   C T F X P K
S B X D H W Q ,   D P A P T G X P K R O
C T B J M   V B X J P N M   S Q B T D K Q
D P J P N X P K   C B Y K K Y N T E X T .

500 RUMMY

Can you score 500 or more points in Word Rummy hands from the card spread below?

ANSWERS, PAGE 128

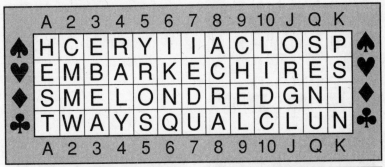

	A	2	3	4	5	6	7	8	9	10	J	Q	K	
♠	H	C	E	R	Y	I	I	A	C	L	O	S	P	♠
♥	E	M	B	A	R	K	E	C	H	I	R	E	S	♥
♦	S	M	E	L	O	N	D	R	E	D	G	N	I	♦
♣	T	W	A	Y	S	Q	U	A	L	C	L	U	N	♣
	A	2	3	4	5	6	7	8	9	10	J	Q	K	

 How to Play

Find as many common seven-letter words as you can whose cards form Word Rummy hands. A Word Rummy hand is a seven-letter word whose letters appear on cards that make up one **set** (three or four cards of a kind, like 7 7 7 or K K K K) and one **sequence** (three or four cards of the same suit in numerical order, like ♥ A 2 3 or ♣ 9 10 J Q). Either the **set** or the **sequence** may come first. The letters of a **set** may be used in any order; the letters of a **sequence** must be used in the left-to-right order given in the grid. The same card cannot be used twice in one hand. Sets and sequences, however, may be repeated in other words. Proper names and foreign words are not allowed, but plurals are fine.

 Scoring

Each card in a Word Rummy hand scores its face value. A 6 scores 6 points, for example. Aces are low and count 1 point each. Jacks, queens, and kings count 10 points each.

 Example

In the puzzle at right the word CLOTHES forms a Word Rummy hand. The ♠ 9 10 J are a sequence with the letters C-L-O; the ♣ A ♠ A ♥ A ♦ A are a set with the letters T-H-E-S. The cards used have values 9 10 10 1 1 1 1, for a total of 33 points.

 Ratings

Knock: 400 points (good game)
Gin: 500 points (winning game)
Gin-off: 983 points (our best score)

CARDS & WORDS	POINTS
C L O T H E S 9 10 J A A A A	33

CARDS & WORDS	POINTS

COLUMN 2 TOTAL	

COLUMN 1 TOTAL	

COLUMN 1 TOTAL	

TOTAL SCORE	

9 PATHFINDER

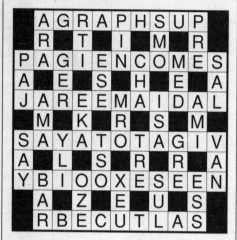

1W	Garage	17N	Made
2W	Artie	18S	Say
3E	Supreme	19W	Take
4W	Pushpin	20S	Vanessa
5S	Tiger	21S	Libya
6S	Inch	22N	Storm
7S	Mocha	22S	Sox
8E	Paragraph	23S	Result
8S	Pajamas	24S	Barbecue
9W	Mom	25W	Oily
10S	Salami	26N	Navigator
11S	Ajar	27N	Zoo
12S	Seek	27S	Zebra
13W	Disagree	28N	Exert
14N	Laser	29N	User
15S	Maya	30E	Cutlass
16N	Siamese		

10 BEEP! BEEP!

H U H	I R A S	S L A M	B O A
A P O	F I F I	H A N A	U R N
H O R N S O F P L E N T Y			L A D
A N N A	S A H A R A		T A L L Y
I N C	I O T A	N A S H	
L E N A H O R N E		L E G H O R N	
O R O	I V E S	G E L S	R O E
M E N A C E	T O O L	S N O W	
H O R N S W O G G L E			
A B B A	L E N O	W I T C H Y	
L I I	C O O L	S P Y S	A R E
F O G H O R N	H O R N P I P E S		
H E L D	D U N E	S T E	
S N O R E	T O L A S T	C H A S	
A I R	T H E M A T T E R H O R N		
I N N	T U N E	A O N E	R N A
L E S	E N D S	S N O B	N O G

11 CRYPTO-FUNNIES 1

Panel 1: How's the assembly going? *Husband*: Lousy.
Panel 2: Don't you want to look at the manual? *Husband*: No!
Panel 3: I've put together a million tricycles in my day!
Panel 4: That's supposed to be a coffee maker.

12 WHAT'S ON TAP?

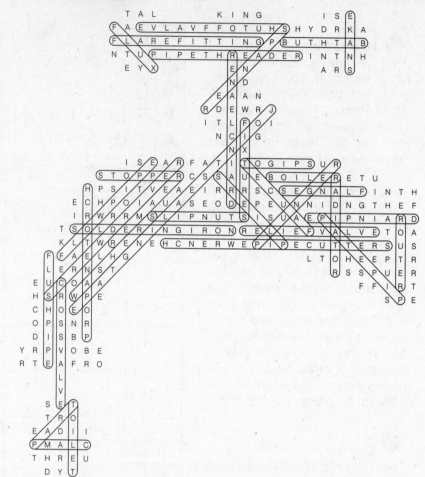

13 PENCIL POINTERS 1

H		P		B			
A L O H A		C O B B L E S T O N E S		
R O M A N N U M E R A L			A L I V E	
K N E L T	P I G O U T		L I N E N	
T E N T H	S T I N G S		E V E N S	
H		E	N T H		E R I E	
T E L E G R A M		E E L S		N	
H E A R	L O G		R A I L I N G S	
E D G E	T O A D		I R O N A G E	
R O L E	A L B U M	R	S A M O A	
J A N E T	R A B B I T S		N E W T	
L		H E L L O		S T E R N S	
D E L T A	D I L U T E			
A X I O M S	N E T		A T B E S T	
N I T W I T S		N		P I R A T E	
G L E N	A C H I N G		L E A V E S	
B E E R S	T R I V I A		A	N E A T	
L	I D E A M A N			S K Y	
S T A D I U M	G	B E G	K	
S O W E D	S N O B	I	A M E N D	
I N A L L	H A T R E D		M A R I A	
N E R V E	A V I A T E		U N I F Y	
G R E E D	W E T T E D		T Y K E S	

16 CLASSIFIED CHAOS

1. Art director
2. Counterperson
3. Proofreader
4. Flight attendant
5. Casting coordinator
6. Plant manager
7. Stock clerk
8. Body damage appraiser
9. Receptionist
10. Filing clerk
11. Cell culture technician
12. Bellman
13. Pressman
14. Field service technician
15. Draftsman

20 EGGS-PECKED-ATIONS

The brown egg, laid by a 9-meter vegetarian Leatherneck, is safe to take. The white egg is laid by a 12-meter vegetarian Giant Leaper. The red-spotted egg is laid by a 13-meter vegetarian Gray Plateback. The blue-spotted egg, laid by an 11-meter carnivorous Ringtail, is the one to avoid.

14 AWARDS NIGHT

```
S E A L E D E N V E L O P E       A C C E P T A N C E
O   C                     M       L       N
N A D   S E   C I N E M A   Y   T O U T   N O   S
G   D   K   D   O       Y   R   M   O   V   O A P
O P E N I N G N U M B E R S   R   Y   Y   U   A P
F   M   T   A   M       S     O   M   O   A   S O
T   Y   A   P R I Z E   B E S T P I C T U R E   R
H   A   G   R   D           R   S   H       D   T A
E   W O   L I   C O U N T R Y M U S I C   L I V E R
Y E A R L Y   I   A   H       K       R E C T   R A
E   R   D   K   A   L O   S U S P E N S E   T   O N
A U D I E N C E   L   O S   W   T   M   S   R   N
R   N   T   L S   O   S C   I   T   A C T R E S S
    F   I   G   O   T   A   N   R O   C   S   O   Y
O   I   G L   O T   N N O U N C E R   I   H O S T
B A L L O T   H O N O R   E   E T   L   O   R   O N
I   M   B   A       R       T   I O   V I C T O R Y
E   B E S T N E W A R T I S T   S       M   E   R
S       S     K           S   S U P P O R T I N G
```

18 INTERNAL LOGIC

```
C A R E ■ S H U N ■ S A D I S T
M O R A Y ■ T O N O ■ A V E N U E
I N T H E C A R D S ■ L I F T E D
A M I ■ S O R R I E R ■ A A H S ■
M A S T ■ A V I D ■ O U N C E ■
I N T H E R E D ■ B A H ■ E B B S
■ ■ A S S ■ V I S O R ■ L O A ■
■ P I T T E D ■ I N T H E D A R K
F I N C H ■ O B E S E ■ L A C E S
I N T H E K N O W ■ D R I N K S ■
D U H ■ R I T A S ■ A S I ■ ■
O P E C ■ E L S ■ I N T H E R A W
■ M A U V E ■ G N A T ■ L A M E ■
■ C O T S ■ T R E A C L E ■ N E D
M O N T H S ■ ■ I N T H E W R O N G
O M E L E T ■ B R I O ■ E A U D E
P A Y E R S ■ S E E S ■ S E T S ■
```

19 QUOTE BOXES

1. "Acting is a matter of giving away secrets. You let the audience crawl inside you for a while."
2. "Thanks to the interstate highway system it is now possible to travel from coast to coast without seeing anything."

19 WORD LADDERS

Our answers (other routes may be possible):
1. PORK, CORK, COOK, COOP, CHOP
2. MEAT, MOAT, MOAN, LOAN, LOAF
3. WISH, WISE, WINE, LINE, LONE, BONE
4. BEEF, BEES, BETS, BATS, BASS, BASH, HASH

15 DOUBLE CROSS 1

A. THE WHITE HOUSE
B. WILDEBEEST
C. ALLOWANCE
D. IT HAPPENED ONE
E. NIGHT
F. MATTER
G. OUTTHRUST
H. RAQUEL WELCH
I. ELVIN HAYES
J. TOGGLE BOLT
K. REGENT
L. AGATHA CHRISTIE
M. MORN
N. POWDER SNOW
O. SHIP OF FOOLS
P. ABBEY ROAD
Q. BUCEPHALUS
R. RENT
S. OTTERHOUND
T. AGITATING
U. DON QUIXOTE

[Coming] in on the equator this noon. A sailor explained to a young girl that the ship's speed is poor because we are climbing up the bulge toward the center of the globe, but that when we ... get over, at the equator, and start downhill, we should fly.—(Mark) Twain, *More Tramps Abroad*

26 SOLITAIRE HANGMAN

I. WRINKLE
II. OBJECTIVE
III. WHISKEY
IV. COPYRIGHT
V. HYPHENATE
VI. BODYGUARD
VII. GYMNASIUM
VIII. QUICKEN
IX. WORKBENCH
X. BOBSLED
XI. SYMPHONY
XII. CHUTZPAH

22 TEXAS LEAGUER

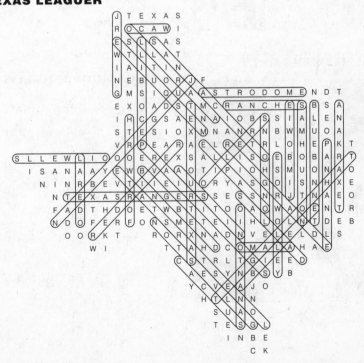

21 WACKY WORDIES

1. Leave no stone unturned
2. Foot in the door
3. Go on a double-date
4. Green with envy
5. Look me square in the eye
6. Broken promise
7. Pull up alongside the curb
8. Excuse me
9. High-grade performance
10. Take on a big job
11. Split the difference
12. He came out of nowhere
13. Wait on hand and foot
14. Suit to a T
15. Know it forward and back
16. A period in history
17. Crooked lawyer
18. Get up on the wrong side of bed
19. Sign on the dotted line
20. Disorderly conduct

24 COMMAND PERFORMANCES

28 FOR MEMBERS ONLY

23 PENCIL POINTERS 2

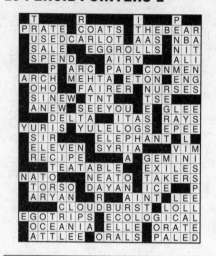

29 CRYPTO-FUNNIES 2

Panel 1: Your work habits are atrocious.
Panel 2: You come in late and go home early.
Panel 3: Come see me at eleven and we'll discuss it.
Panel 4: What, and miss breakfast?

31 BEYOND THE PALE

1. Snow White
2. White Sox
3. The White House
4. Vanna White
5. White elephant
6. White sale
7. White lightning
8. Bobwhite
9. "(I'm Dreaming of a) White Christmas"
10. Perry White
11. White lie
12. The White Rabbit
13. *White Fang*
14. Paul Whiteman

30 HOOP HOOP HOORAY!

25 DOUBLE CROSS 2

A. GAWAIN
B. EINSTEIN
C. ODDS
D. ROD CAREW
E. GATS
F. EDSEL FORD
G. MUTTON
H. INSTITUTION
I. KANSAS CITY
J. EDITS
K. SPITTOON
L. HOBBITS
M. OUTSTAY
N. WHIRLAWAY
O. THE MERCHANT
P. OF VENICE
Q. BE MY BABY
R. EURYTION
S. AMADEUS
T. NORMAN MAILER
U. AFTEREFFECTS
V. LOUDON
W. INFAMOUS
X. EUROPEANS
Y. NATTY

In England it is bad manners ... to assert something confidently. It may be your personal view that two and two make four, but you must not state it in a self-assured way, because this is a democratic country, and others may be of a different opinion.—George Mikes, *How to Be an Alien*

31 CROSS ANAGRAM

32 LOOSE CHANGE

33 PENCIL POINTERS 3

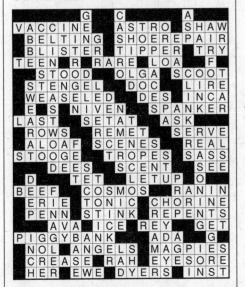

34 ABSOLUTELY BATTY

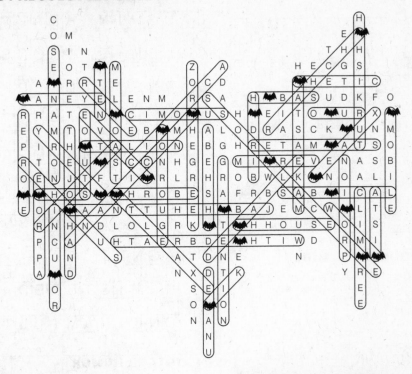

35 DOUBLE CROSS 3

A. BOB NEWHART
B. EMMANUEL
C. NOW, VOYAGER
D. NUISANCES
E. EDMONTON
F. TIP-OFF
G. TEAS
H. COCHISE
I. ELI WALLACH
J. RIMINI
K. FIFTIES
L. TO A TEE
M. ROMMEL
N. YANKEE DOODLE
O. ARGONAUTS
P. NAPALM
Q. DEATHTRAP
R. SHEEPISH
S. THE DOCK
T. OF THE BAY
U. PHYLUM
V. MUMMIES
W. ELLERY QUEEN

Emily Wedge of Baltimore's famous Enoch Pratt Library quotes a gentleman who declared, "My wife says I have had tee many martoonis, but I am not so much under the allfuence of incohol as some pinkle theep. I mean *thinkle peep*."—Bennett Cerf, *Try and Stop Me*

36 JUMBO CROSSWORD 1

38 DSZQUPHSBNT! 1

1. CRYPTOON. "Very sorry, sir...This lifetime warranty clearly states it's only valid for the life of the watch."
2. THAT'S IT? Success to me is having ten honeydew melons and eating only the top half of each one. — Barbra Streisand
3. WRONG SIZE. A cheerful clerk sits at the Christmas gift exchange counter, wishing everyone many "happy returns."
4. I'LL TOO. The new spelling bee champ, sent shopping by her mom, can't find "Froot Loops," "Ty-D-bol," or "Reddi wip."
5. NIGHT VISION. Old man places toupee, bifocals, and dentures on table before bed; nearsighted wife thinks his head has fallen off.
6. JUSTICE? Jaded judge jolts jury, jabbering, "Just jeer jaywalkers, jail johns, jettison junkies."
7. LOOK AT THE TIME! Showy child belts lousy tunes while proud folks nudge weary guest, "Aren't these great, Frank?"

39 JIGSAW BOXES

The Aruwimi River in Zaire was named by the explorer Livingstone. On discovering it, he asked a native, "What is this river's name?" The native replied, "Aruwimi," meaning "What is this man saying?" Livingstone misunderstood and the river has been the Aruwimi ever since.

40 INT'L BREAKFAST

```
OPENER STORMS EDT
MOTIVE COVERS NEO
SPANISHOMELET GNU
   ALTAR RID BLUR
JOB SUSPECT GLIDE
AREA PHILA ERASED
BILGE OKS RASH
BOGEYMAN TRANSMIT
ELI EON OTT USE
DEADLINE STOODFOR
 NEIL GEM RIFLE
REWEDS GREEK KIDS
OMARS SPELLER NEA
LIFE GIL LINUS
ALF CANADIANBACON
NIL AVENUE ELMORE
DOE PESTER LESSEE
```

41 DOUBLE FEATURES

1. *Apocalypse Now / Broadcast News*
2. *Blazing Saddles / National Velvet*
3. *The Birds / True Grit*
4. *Giant / Shane*
5. *Marathon Man / The Graduate*
6. *Rear Window / Wall Street*
7. *Casablanca / Moonstruck*
8. *Bonnie and Clyde / Fatal Attraction*
9. *Catch-22 / La Bamba*
10. *American Graffiti / Coming to America*
11. *RoboCop / Tin Men*
12. *Dial M for Murder / Full Metal Jacket*
13. *A Chorus Line / Dirty Dancing*
14. *Married to the Mob / The Princess Bride*
15. *M*A*S*H / Platoon*

43 DOUBLE CROSS 4

A. RITTER
B. ALICE'S RESTAURANT
C. CITATION
D. HOWARD FAST
E. ERROL FLYNN
F. LIFFEY
G. COFFEEWEED
H. AUNTIE MAME
I. RENT
J. STOWE
K. OF MICE AND MEN
L. NUTRITION
M. SPEED-THE-PLOW
N. ISLAMABAD
O. LINT
P. EASY RIDER
Q. NATURE
R. TWO WOMEN
S. STEINWAY
T. PINAFORE
U. RIOT
V. INDUSTRY
W. NOTIFIES
X. GUIDRY

Our attitude toward plants is a singularly narrow one. If we see any immediate utility in a plant we foster it. If for any reason we find its presence undesirable or merely a matter of indifference, we may condemn it to destruction forthwith.—Rachel Carson, *Silent Spring*

42 DÉJÀ VU

```
LAUGHIN   REALMCCOYS      NEWHART
VALERIE  IRONSIDE   BRADYBUNCH
BARNEYMILLER  STARTREK
ALICE   BONANZA   HARRYO
SLEDGEHAMMER  DAKTARI   MASH
NATEAM        TAXI    OUTSIDER
      GUNSMOKE
DRAGNET            BONANZA
       DRAGNET     EQUALIZER
    MISTERED
   ONEINAMILLION  FAME  CHEERS
```

44 VINTAGE HUMOR

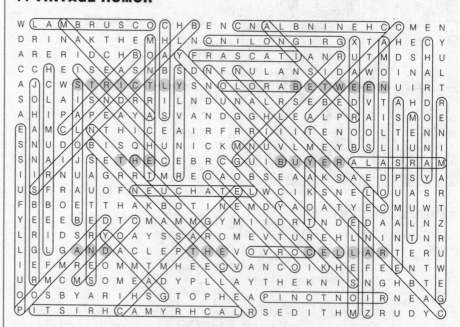

The completed joke is: "The price of a good wine is strictly between the buyer and the cellar."

51 CRYPTO-FUNNIES 3

Panel 1: We made it! *Henchman*: Yeah, Boss!
Panel 2: Okay, where's the loot? *Henchman*: I handed it all out on the corner . . . like you told me to.
Panel 3: Like I told you to?! *Henchman*: Sure—you said, "Time to make our big giveaway!"
Panel 4: Close.

55 A+

1. A-broad
2. A-maze
3. A-gent
4. A-tone
5. A-muse
6. A-gain
7. A-mount
8. A-trophy
9. A-bout
10. A-jar
11. A-scent
12. A-bridge
13. A-verse
14. A-ren(')t

45 PENCIL POINTERS 4

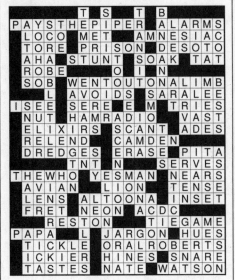

Crossword grid answers include:
PAYSTHEPIPER, ALARMS, LOCO, MET, AMNESIAC, TORE, PRISON, DESOTO, AHA, STUNT, SOAK, TAT, ROBE, SOB, WENTOUTONALIMB, AVOIDS, SARALEE, ISEE, SERE, TRIES, NUT, HAMRADIO, VAST, ELIXIRS, SCANT, ADES, RELEND, CAMDEN, DREDGES, ERASE, PITA, TNT, SERVES, THEWHO, YESMAN, NEARS, AVIAN, LION, TENSE, LENS, ALTOONA, INSET, FRET, NEON, ACDC, RESTON, TIEGAME, PAPA, JARGON, HUES, TICKLE, ORALROBERTS, ICKIER, HINES, SNARE, TASTES, NATE, WATSON

48 SO LONG

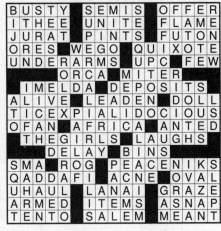

Crossword grid answers include:
BUSTY, SEMIS, OFFER, ITHEE, UNITE, FLAME, JURAT, PINTS, FUTON, ORES, WEGO, QUIXOTE, UNDERARMS, UPC, FEW, ORCA, MITER, IMELDA, DEPOSITS, ALIVE, LEADEN, DOLL, TICEXPIALIDOCIOUS, OFAN, AFRICA, ANTED, THEGIRLS, LAUGHS, DELAY, BINS, SMA, ROG, PEACENIKS, QADDAFI, ACNE, OVAL, UHAUL, LANAI, GRAZE, ARMED, ITEMS, ASNAP, TENTO, SALEM, MEANT

56 SCRAMBLED COMICS

TAKE YOUR PICK: E, A, G, C, B, D, F
WHEN SIDNEY MET SHIRLEY: F, C, A, E, G, D, B
BOYS WILL BE BOYS: F, D, A, E, B, C, G

46 HEAD HUNTING

1.
2.
3.
4.
5.
6.
7.
8.

53 DOUBLE CROSS 5

A. GRAND
B. EDDIE MONEY
C. OSCAR
D. FATHERHOOD
E. FATAL BEAUTY
F. RAPPEL
G. ELIE WIESEL
H. YOU'RE SO FINE
I. HALF-MAST
J. UPTON SINCLAIR
K. GHANA
L. HADES
M. ESCUTCHEON
N. STROLL
O. WRIST
P. OFF-LIMITS
Q. ROBERT DUVALL
R. DACCA
S. SHAFT
T. INCAS
U. NARROWS
V. THE TOMMYKNOCKERS
W. INVISIBLE TOUCH
X. MEND
Y. EAST COAST

[English vocabulary] reflects the main social developments of the past thousand years in profound ... and fascinating ways. If all the main historical sources ... had been lost, the word-stock itself would remain a remarkably accurate record of those times.—Geoffrey Hughes, *Words in Time*

52 SIGNS OF TROUBLE

The signs are positioned as shown below.

49 THE SPIRAL

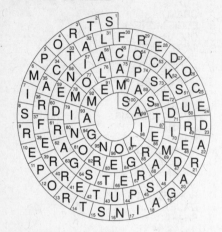

50 DIRTY WORDS

54 PENCIL Y'S

65 LIMBERICKS

1. Owned, groaned, beau, crow, unstoned
2. Obsessed, chest, admits, spitz, distressed
3. Schools, fools, prohibits, kibitz, rules

58 HIDE & SEEK

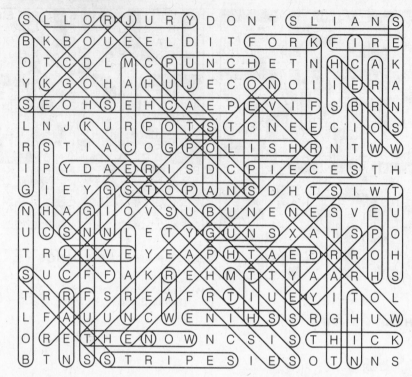

59 SPLIT DECISIONS

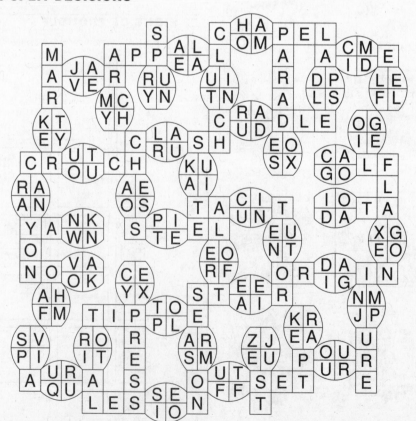

60 CRYPTOLISTS

1. Children of Literature
Peter Pan
Christopher Robin
Eloise
Tiny Tim
Pippi Longstocking
Oliver Twist
Huckleberry Finn
Heidi
Little Lord Fauntleroy
Pinocchio

2. Found in a Newspaper
Sports section
Movie listings
"Help wanted"
Letters to the Editor
Comics
Restaurant reviews
Headlines
Weather reports
Stock prices
Horoscope

3. Food Inseparables
Spaghetti & meatballs
Peanut butter & jelly
Milk & cookies
Fish & chips
Bacon & eggs
Ham & cheese
Franks & beans
Bread & butter
Lettuce & tomato
Meat & potatoes

4. Mystery List
(Things that have frames)
Eyeglasses
Bowling game
Window
Wooden house
Automobile
Graduation photo
Bed
Motion picture film
Comic strip
Bicycle

61 PENCIL POINTERS 5

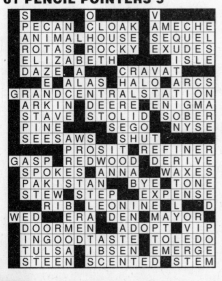

62 BASKET CASE

Lettie's last visit, requiring all right forks (clue 2), was to cottage E. The first two cottages she visited were the only two whose access routes begin with a left fork: A and B (clue 4). Cousin Lila's cottage, accessed by two consecutive left forks (clue 7), must be C. The visit to the cousin's cottage, C, which succeeded the visits to both grandmas (clue 1) and to the aunt in clue 4, must have come fourth.

It follows that the first and third visits were to the two grandmas: the former offered the fruitcake (clue 4), and the latter, who lived, by elimination, in cottage D, offered the apple cobbler (clue 1). The last visit was not to Aunt Lotta (clue 3) but to Aunt Laura; the second visit was to Aunt Lotta. Since cottage E (the only one with an access route that uses no left forks) is Aunt Laura's, Grandma Redhood's and Grandma Ryding's cottages are accessed by one and two left forks, respectively (clue 6). They must be D and A, and Aunt Lotta's cottage is B. The cherry cheesecake, given by neither aunt (clue 5), was given by Cousin Lila. The chocolate torte, not Aunt Lotta's gift (clue 3), was from Aunt Laura. Aunt Lotta's gift, by elimination, was the almond bundt cake.

In summary, by order of visit:
1. Cottage A, Grandma Ryding, fruitcake
2. Cottage B, Aunt Lotta, almond bundt cake
3. Cottage D, Grandma Redhood, apple cobbler
4. Cottage C, Cousin Lila, cherry cheesecake
5. Cottage E, Aunt Laura, chocolate torte

63 DOUBLE CROSS 6

A. KENNETH GRAHAME
B. I LIKE IKE
C. NATHAN HALE
D. GUTTED
E. SWEET POTATOES
F. OUTFITTED
G. LADYSMITH
H. VESTED
I. EXHAUST
J. RAPACIOUS
K. TAJ MAHAL
L. HUTCHINSON
M. EGG WHITES
N. BOWWOW
O. ELBOW
P. ANDREW WYETH
Q. NOMADIC
R. TATTER
S. RIDDLE
T. EIGHTH
U. EUPHEMISM
V. SETH THOMAS

There were two things about Mama ... she always expected the best out of me.... then no matter what I did, whatever I came home with, she acted like it was the moon I had just hung up in the sky and plugged in all the stars. Like I was that good.—(Barbara) Kingsolver, *The Bean Trees*

64 OFF WITH THEIR HEADS!

66 CRYPTIC CROSSWORD 1

ACROSS
1 Resist (sister)
4 Step on it (set point)
9 Alike (Al + Ike)
10 Mistermed (m + Mister Ed)
11 Pago Pago (p. + ago + p. + ago)
12 Weasel (w + easel)
14 Adam (a + dam)
15 Idolater (I do + later)
19 Sinister (sister + in)
20 Emit (*Time*)
23 Lyrics (Cyril's)
25 Nintendo (no + intend)
27 Manacling (man + a + cling)
28 Plain (plan + I)
29 Soybeans (by one ass)
30 Trashy (try + ash)

DOWN
1 Reappear (reap + pear)
2 Stingrays (S + tins + gray)
3 Sleepy (Lee + spy)
5 Toss (to + SS)
6 Presents (serpents)
7 Names (N + Ames)
8 Toddle (geT ODD LEtters)
10 Megadose (E + soda + gem)
13 Altering (triangle)
16 Romanians (Ron's + mania)
17 Unicycle (uncle + icy)
18 Attorney (a tourney)
21 Llamas (a + small)
22 Stupor (Proust)
24 Rangy (angry)
26 Lion (milLIONs)

71 CRYPTO-FUNNIES 4

Panel 1: Isn't that where Jeffy Byrd lives? *Girl*: Yup.
Panel 2: Why are they moving?
Panel 3: His dad's a beekeeper. The neighbors kept complaining. *Boy*: Wow!
Panel 4: Hey—I just found out about the Byrds and the bees!

ANSWERS

67 ALPHABET CITY

A Austin, TX
B Baltimore, MD
C Chicago, IL
D Detroit, MI
E El Paso, TX
F Fort Worth, TX
G Grand Rapids, MI
H Houston, TX
I Indianapolis, IN
J Jacksonville, FL
K Kansas City, MO
L Los Angeles, CA
M Milwaukee, WI
N New York, NY
O Oklahoma City, OK
P Philadelphia, PA
Q Quincy, MA
R Rochester, NY
S San Diego, CA
T Tucson, AZ
U Utica, NY
V Virginia Beach, VA
W Washington, DC
X Xenia, OH
Y Yonkers, NY
Z Zanesville, OH

Ratings

23-26   Splendid perspicacity
17-22   Remarkable sagacity
10-16   Notable tenacity
Under 10   Geographical incapacity

73 DOUBLE CROSS 7

A. BILLIONAIRE
B. OFFEND
C. MOTIF
D. BONN
E. ENTENTE
F. CASTAWAY
G. KIEV
H. A HARD DAY'S NIGHT
I. UPROAR
J. NOUGAT
K. TENDER
L. EYESORE
M. RAVIOLI
N. MANET
O. ANTIHERO
P. SEDER
Q. CHIFFON
R. OF THEE I SING
S. PARSIMONY
T. EIDER
U. BUFFER
V. OATH
W. ORTEGA
X. KLINGON

There is no known navy blue food of any kind. If there is any navy blue food in the refrigerator it signifies death. Also, an open refrigerator door and the furnace going at the same time are incompatible.—(Erma) Bombeck, *Aunt Erma's Cope Book*

70 NOT ALL THERE

Gospel writers: Mark, Luke, John; missing: Matthew
Colors: red, orange, yellow, green, blue, violet; missing: indigo
Charlie's Angels: (Farrah) Fawcett-Majors, (Kate) Jackson, (Cheryl) Ladd, (Tanya) Roberts, (Shelley) Hack; missing: (Jaclyn) Smith
Seasons: summer, autumn, winter; missing: spring
Oceans: Atlantic, Pacific, Arctic, Antarctic; missing: Indian
Planets: Mercury, Venus, Earth, Mars, Jupiter, Saturn, Uranus, Pluto; missing: Neptune
Dwarfs: Doc, Dopey, Sleepy, Sneezy, Happy, Bashful; missing: Grumpy
The initials of the items left out spell MISSING.

78 PAIRAGRAMS

1. Norse snore
2. Steno notes
3. Hiker's shriek
4. Serpent present
5. Garden danger
6. Nameless salesmen
7. Trout tutor
8. Oriental relation
9. Solemn lemons
10. Amused Medusa
11. Goats' togas
12. Noiseless lionesses

68 JUMBO CROSSWORD 2

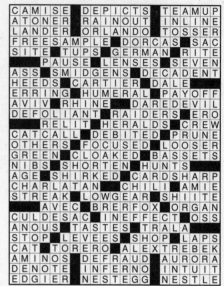

72 BATHDAY WISH

74 "C" HERE

| C O N C E R T | | C H A R C O A L | | C O D | | C R O C U S |

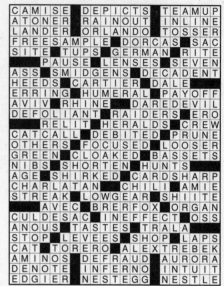

75 PENCIL POINTERS 6

77 SIAMESE TWINS

76 FOR MYSTERY LOVERS

81 DOUBLE CROSS 8

A. RAIN DANCE
B. OSTENTATIOUS
C. GETTYSBURG
D. EFFUSIVE
E. RODEO
F. KHYBER PASS
G. ANSWER
H. HONED
I. NOODLE
J. TORTE
K. HENRY CLAY
L. EBONY
M. BLACK HOLE
N. ORDINATION
O. YELLOW FEVER
P. SKUNKED
Q. OXFORD
R. FRIDAY
S. SPOON RIVER
T. UNSTABLE
U. MANDALAY
V. MORTON SALT
W. EGGPLANT
X. RIBBON

As far as anyone knows, the nickname proceeded from benign absurdity. Brooklyn, being flat, extensive, and populous, was an early stronghold of the trolley car. Enter absurdity. To survive in Brooklyn one had to be a dodger of trolleys.—Roger Kahn, *The Boys of Summer*

83 LABYRINTH

82 DSZQUPHSBNT! 2

1. CRYPTOON. Come quick! The couple that did so badly on "The Newlywed Game" is now on "Divorce Court!"

2. QUITE A LIKENESS. "There is a reason people look the way they do. The face one wears has been earned through perseverance."—Al Hirschfeld

3. SO LONG, AGO. The term "good-bye" was etymologically whittled down from the one-time farewell "God be with ye."

4. SIMPLE DEDUCTION. Sherlock, examining empty grave, tells Watson, "There's an underhanded undertaker underfoot—understand?"

5. STICK UP. When peanut butter and jelly trucks collided, one driver shouted, "Help me get out of this jam!" The reply: "In a jif!"

6. GLUG, GLUG. Aquatic athlete says now-stagnant career started out swimmingly, took a dive, went down the drain.

7. ENVIRONMENTAL WARNING. Great treed areas, today being razed, might upset vital ozone layer later, doing Earth havoc.

86 CROSS-EXAMINATION

80 ANYTOWN, USA

85 RIGHTANGLES

#1—Fill-In

B	O	R	E	A	S	E	L
I	O	Z	W	S	T	I	F
C	T	O	H	S	P	A	F
Y	R	I	E	L	M	R	A
D	A	U	H	O	U	T	R
N	U	Q	T	G	J	A	M
A	R	N	O	L	C	N	U
L	A	I	N	A	R	E	S

#2—Square Deal

Q	S	I	R	E	D	U	T
U	O	A	P	I	N	O	C
E	L	S	A	N	A	C	H
B	I	T	T	E	G	S	L
R	T	A	I	R	E	D	E
I	D	G	E	N	C	E	G
O	N	E	P	I	K	N	I
R	E	K	O	D	S	T	S

84 SIGNIFICANT OTHERS

The sun signs and rising signs of the three men and three women—who were paired off into three couples—together comprise the 12 zodiacal signs. Ms. Ramm has her sun in a water sign (clue 1); a second woman has her sun in (the earth sign) Capricorn (clue 8); and a third woman, April, has an air sign and a fire sign (clue 5). The woman with (the water sign) Pisces rising (clue 2) is either Ms. Ramm or the one with her sun in Capricorn: If the latter were the woman with both signs of the same element (both earth), then Ms. Ramm's rising sign would be Pisces and both her signs water—which would contradict clue 3. Hence, Ms. Ramm has two water signs and Pisces rising. By elimination, Ms. Ramm is Mae, and June is the Capricorn (clue 3). June was paired with Janus (clue 8). By elimination, Mae was paired with Julio (clue 1) and April with Mario; and Julio is Bulley (clue 2). Mario's sun sign—water, but not Scorpio (clues 1, 5)—is Cancer, and Mae's sun sign is Scorpio. Since the one with sun in (the earth sign) Taurus is a man, Fishman is June, and the former is Janus (clue 6). Julio has (the fire sign) Aries rising, and Ms. Goatz—who, by elimination of women, is April—has (the air sign) Gemini rising (clue 7). By elimination of last names, Crabbe is a man. Since April's sun sign must be a fire sign (clue 5), (the air sign) Libra is June's rising sign and Crabbe is Janus—whose rising sign is Aquarius (clue 4). Lions, by elimination, is Mario. The three signs not yet accounted for are Leo, Sagittarius, and (the earth sign) Virgo. Virgo, neither April's nor Mario's (clue 5), is Julio's sun sign; Mario's rising sign, not Leo (clue 9), is Sagittarius; and, by elimination, Leo is April's sun sign.

In summary: Julio Bulley (sun in Virgo, Aries rising) and Mae Ramm (sun in Scorpio, Pisces rising)

Janus Crabbe (sun in Taurus, Aquarius rising) and June Fishman (sun in Capricorn, Libra rising)

Mario Lions (sun in Cancer, Sagittarius rising) and April Goatz (sun in Leo, Gemini rising).

87 PENCIL POINTERS 7

88 PIONEERING PUZZLES

1. In the engraving below, more detail has been added to make the profiles obvious:

2. "Think twice before you speak once" (TH in K twice, before U's, P E A, K on CE)
3. "All's well that ends well" (awls, wealth, at, ends, well)
4. Careful examination shows that Brown did not kill *Brooks*, but *13 rooks*, which does not constitute murder.
5. If you hold the page horizontally almost at eye level, an elongated figure appears among the words "WHO IS IT?" Turning the page 90° clockwise and reading in the same manner, the answer appears: "OUR FUNNY EDITOR IN HIS SANCTUM."
6. Here is one solution; others are possible.

94 DANCE PARTIES

90 CRYPTIC CROSSWORD 2

ACROSS

1 Junks (two meanings)
4 Escalates (late + cases)
9 X-raying (X + in gray)
10 Nominal (veNOM IN A Lecture)
11 Avenge (Geneva)
12 Benefits (bets + fine)
14 Outlandish (lout and his)
15 Prom (PeRfOrM)
18 East (beast – b)
20 Monotonous (sun to moon + O)
23 Thematic (a + tic + them)
24 Appear (a peer)
26 Unleash (uncle – c + has)
27 Rhubarb (R + hu + barb)
28 Haciendas (I dance + has)
29 Drove (two meanings)

DOWN

1 Juxtapose (Expo just a)
2 Neatest (eat + nest)
3 Stingray (straying)
4 Ergo (ogre)
5 Conversion (con + version)
6 Lumber (two meanings)
7 Tangier (two meanings)
8 Sales (sails)
13 Admonished (diamond + she)
16 Miserable (bares + mile)
17 Compound (come – e + pound)
19 Shellac (she + call)
21 Oregano (nag + Oreo)
22 Palace (place + a)
23 Truth (truce)
25 Urns (turns – t)

93 CRYPTO-FUNNIES 5

Panel 1: How's the water, hon? *Woman*: Great!
Panel 2: Holy mackerel! I've never been this cold in my life! How did she stand it?
Panel 3: I thought you said the water was great! *Woman*: It is!
Panel 4: Have some!

96 ABOUT FACE

91 DOUBLE CROSS 9

A. WHEEDLE
B. E. L. DOCTOROW
C. LONDON
D. THINNER
E. YAHWEH
F. ONION FIELD
G. NUTHATCH
H. ELENI
I. WHELK
J. ROSA PARKS
K. INTUITS
L. TEETOTALER
M. EDITH WHARTON
N. RIFFRAFF
O. SEMANTICS
P. BLOOMERS
Q. ENOCH
R. GOGOL
S. IVORY TOWERS
T. NOMINATE
U. NEMATODE
V. INFEST
W. NAPALM
X. GHETTO
Y. SHREVE

Writing fiction has developed in me an abiding respect for the unknown in a human lifetime and a sense of where to look for the threads, how to follow, how to connect …. The strands are all there: To the memory nothing is ever really lost.—(Eudora) Welty, *One Writer's Beginnings*

104 REBUS RIOT WORD LIST

The words in order are:

ABANDON (AB and ON)
ABYSMALLY (A by small Y)
AVOIDED (A voided)
BELITTLED (BE little D)
BLUNDERBUSS (BL under BUSS)
BYGONES (by G, one S)
CAMPGROUND (CAMPG round)
CLOVERLEAF (CL over LEAF)
CONDONE (C on D on E)
COUPONS (CO upon S)
DISCOVERY (D is C over Y)
FLASHBACK (FLASH back)
GRANDPARENTS (GR and P aren't S)
HALF-LIFE (half LIFE)
HANDICAPS (H and I cap S)
HOVERCRAFT (H over CRAFT)
IMPOVERISH (IMP over ISH)
LABYRINTH (LA by R in TH)
LACROSSE (L across E)
LOCKUP (LOCK up)
MIXTURE (mix TURE)
NAUGHTY (naught Y)
NETWORKS (NE two RKs)
PARTHENON (PAR, then ON)
PINOCHLE (P in OCHLE)
PRINTOUT (PR into UT)
RAFTERS (R after S)
SANDSTONE (S and ST on E)
SATURATE (S at UR at E)
SHOWDOWN (SHOW down)
SONNET (S on NET)
SPRINTED (S printed)
THUNDERCLAP (TH under CLAP)
TRICERATOPS (TRICER atop S)
TRIPLET (triple T)
WHEREWITHAL (W here with AL)

92 WAY TO GO!

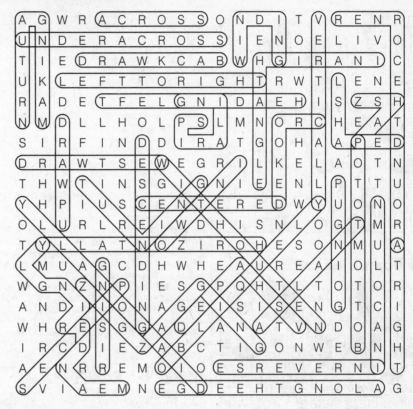

95 HEX SIGNS

The completed sentences are:

1. The tennis player later felT REMORse for not shaking his opponent's hand.
2. If you aren't quiet in your apartment, you maynot be offered a leaSE RENEwal.
3. A pathological liAR IS ESpecially likely to commit perjury on witness stands.
4. The biology major used faulty gramMAR IN Essays about creatures of the sea.
5. In the Far East, it's not unusual to shaRE MOTEl rooms with total strangers.
6. A group of poliCEMEN Thwarted the thief, one using his night stick.
7. The teacher and her clASS ENTered into an agreement on assignments.
8. At the wedding, the groom's couSIN GEStured for the guests to raise their glasses for toasts.
9. The begGAR DENied stealing any tomatoes from the small vegetable patch.
10. I truly hoPE RIO De Janeiro isn't too exciting for a person my age.
11. You can tell that belly danCER IS Embarrassed by her bright red face.
12. After only one drink, it becomes difficult to conNECT A Rope to a hitching post.
13. The singer didn't know whether to sing what he'd originally choSEN OR Another verse of "Lady of Spain."
14. Julian painted his VolkswAGEN DArk blue with slate gray trim.
15. Dancers of the tANGO RArely wear wool, since it would get too hot.
16. The whole orchestra was kicked out of the hotel after the woodwind player got toO BOISTerous.
17. All but the fiNEST LEather belts may curl up after years of use.
18. Because of his basiC ORNERiness, the crook refused to surrender to the authorities.
19. The chief detective on the caSE CONDucted a thorough investigation from the moment he entered.
20. First-time bowlers may need guiDANCE Selecting their bowling balls.
21. When asked why he ate so much, the glutTON SILently indicated he had something in his throat.
22. The archvillain loved to call people names purely foR EVIL Effect.
23. The sharp end of a raPIER CErtainly could penetrate a dueler's thick coat.
24. The banker asked our print shop to typESET ANother copy of his foreign currency exchange rates.

98 MY FIRST CASE

102 BOXING MATCH

P A R M A		P L A T E		A C O S T

Box answers: A. Contessa B. Solstice C. Ocarinas D. Serenade E. Tenspots F. Adelaide G. Resonant

Puzzle dedicatee: Pandora

108 RIDDLE-DE-DEE

Answer to the riddle: The monk is a little faster.

100 SWEET EIGHTEEN

The hazelnut is mentioned in clue 1 and clue 6. Fix its place (it doesn't matter which section you start with), with the lemon jelly two groups counterclockwise (clue 6). If the almond, flanked by hazelnut and orange jelly (clue 1), is placed counterclockwise from the hazelnut, the lemon and orange jellies will occupy the same group. Therefore, the almond is clockwise from the hazelnut—with the orange jelly and the maple cream two groups counterclockwise from the hazelnut (clues 1 and 6).

The peanut cannot go in the group with the hazelnut, the almond, the maple cream/orange jelly (for it must have the raspberry jelly two groups counterclockwise), or the group opposite the hazelnut (for it must be immediately clockwise of mocha cream (clue 4)). If the peanut joins the lemon jelly, it will have mocha cream immediately counterclockwise; and raspberry jelly will join the hazelnut (clue 4). Now there is only one spot for marshmallow cream: between hazelnut and lemon jelly/peanut, with mint jelly joining mocha cream/cashew, and pecan joining maple cream/orange jelly. Now there is only one way for the strawberry jelly to be opposite the vanilla cream (clue 5): by having the strawberry jelly join the almond; but if it does, it will have to share the only spot remaining for the strawberry cream (by the alignment in clue 2),

and this violates clue 7. Therefore, the peanut does not join the lemon jelly.

The only spot for the peanut is between the hazelnut and the lemon jelly. This leaves just two possibilities for the marshmallow cream (from clue 2): joining the peanut or joining the almond/raspberry jelly. But in the latter case, there will be no way to align the apple jelly (clue 3). So the only place for marshmallow is with peanut; pecan joins maple cream/orange jelly, and mint jelly goes opposite hazelnut. Now the only way to have vanilla cream and strawberry jelly opposite (clue 5) is having vanilla cream join mint jelly. All jellies but one are now aligned, so by elimination, apple jelly joins peanut/marshmallow cream. By elimination, chocolate cream goes with hazelnut/strawberry jelly; and likewise, walnut goes with lemon jelly/mocha cream.

In summary: clockwise, starting at any section, the candies are grouped together in the following order:

	CREAMS	JELLIES	NUTS
Group 1	Chocolate	Strawberry	Hazelnut
Group 2	Strawberry	Raspberry	Almond
Group 3	Maple	Orange	Pecan
Group 4	Vanilla	Mint	Cashew
Group 5	Mocha	Lemon	Walnut
Group 6	Marshmallow	Apple	Peanut

97 DOUBLE CROSS 10

A. BOWWOW
B. EYETEETH
C. NEGATING
D. CHANGE OF SCENERY
E. HELTER SKELTER
F. LETHARGY
G. EMPHATIC
H. YAMAMOTO
I. LIFELINE
J. OSSIFYING
K. STOMACHS
L. TAXONOMY
M. ANTIMATTER
N. NEWSPAPERS
O. DINGOES
P. FIFTY-FIFTY
Q. ORCHESTRATING
R. ULTERIOR MOTIVE
S. NATCH
T. DWARF STARS

I always find myself alone at a race, having become separated from the rest of my party shortly after entering....One of my few excitements at horse racing is seeing how long I can stick with the rest of my party without getting lost.—(Robert Benchley), *Benchley, Lost and Found*

101 POLISH YOUR WITS

1. A Switch in Time Saves Nine

5	0	7
6	4	2
1	8	3

The 9 is turned upside-down to become a 6. Each row, column, and diagonal totals 12.

2. Don't Worry, Be Happy

```
      1
    1 4
  1 1 5
+ 4 1 5
  5 4 5
```

Note: In the first and third columns, the 1's and 4's may be interchanged.

3. Squaring Up

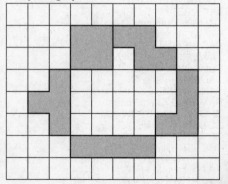

103 CHANGE PLACES

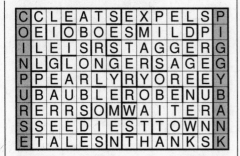

ACROSS: 1. Pleats (pastel) 5. Excels (ex + C + els) 9. Obies (Boise) 10. Mold (two meanings) 11. Legs (gel + s) 12. Stagier (is great) 13. Logger (lager) 14. Sane (an + SE) 16. Yearly (y + early) 18. Pore (two meanings) 20. Babble (bale + BB) 23. Roue (rue + 0) 27. Eras (a + ERs) 28. Writer (righter) 29. Neediest (diet seen) 30. Tows (sot + w) 31. Talks (stalk) 32. Thanes (hasten).

DOWN: 1. Cell (sell) 2. Liege (e.g. + lie) 3. Absorbs (a + B + S + orbs) 4. Torn (to + RN) 5. Ester (Esther) 6. Pigs (sPrInG iS) 7. Elgar (large) 8. Spree (per se) 10. Mary (army) 13. Laurel (allure) 15. Gene (judGE NEver) 17. Yemen (yen + me) 19. Obit (O + bit) 20. Best (be + St.) 21. Area (are + a) 22. Lois (is + L + O) 24. Oath (at + oh) 25. Eton (note) 26. Urns (earns)

106 ABRIDGED DICTIONARY

The dictionary entries defined or illustrated in each excerpt are as follows:

1. Hots; hot seat; hot spring; Hottentot; hot tub; hot up; hot war; hot water; hound
2. Amoeba; amole; among; amontillado; amoral
3. Foregone; foregone conclusion; foreground; foregut; forehand
4. Reign; reign of terror; reimburse; rein; reincarnate; reincarnation; reindeer
5. Flaming; flamingo; flammability
6. Easter; Easter egg; Easter lily
7. Proofreaders' marks; proper
8. Timeworn; time zone
9. Element; elephant
10. Zodiac
11. According to; accordion; accost; accouchement; accoucheur; account
12. Slotback; slot car; sloth
13. Möbius strip; mobocracy; mobster; moccasin
14. Rapid; rapid eye movement; rapid-fire; rapidity; rapid transit; rapier; rapine
15. Run; rune

30 HOOP HOOP HOORAY! HINT

The first word across is CHAMBERLAIN.

42 DÉJÀ VU HINT

The first word across is LAUGH-IN.

74 "C" HERE HINT

The first word across is CONCERT.

104 REBUS RIOT

105 ONE, TWO, THREE

F	AL	CON		MO	T	O	R		CAM	E	R	AS
AR	CHE	S		R	I	C	ES		OU	TH	OU	SES
CE	M	ENT		SEC	RE	TAG	ENT		FL	AN	GE	S
S	IST	ER	HO	OD		ON	S	T	AGE			
			R	E	MUS		HOU	S	EAR	RE	ST	
S	P	IN	S		CO	PYR	I	GHT		TH	IN	E
LO	A	V	ES		VIT	AMI	NC		RA	W	DE	AL
PE	RC	ENT		SW	E	D	EN		INF	ORM	ER	S
S	H	OR	TH	AND		SE	ASH	ORE				
			R	IVE	T	S		WE	ST	PO	IN	T
DEL	A	WAR	E		RE	LA	NE	D		S	TO	IC
I	NI	TI	ATE		AT	T	U	NES		THA	N	K
S	TA	ME	NS		Y	ES	TER	DAY		STE	E	LER

111 MARCHING BANDS

P	O	S	S	E	S	S	I	N	G	L	E	D
S	P	I	L	L	A	G	E	R	I	N	S	E
E	N	T	E	R	R	E	I	N	D	E	E	R
C	I	N	E	R	A	M	A	F	I	N	C	H
A	L	A	D	D	I	N	G	R	O	T	T	O
P	U	R	E	E	S	C	H	A	S	S	I	S
T	S	E	T	S	E	■	E	V	O	L	V	E
I	N	T	E	R	L	U	D	E	A	E	O	N
S	I	E	V	E	S	H	O	R	R	O	R	S
N	O	V	O	C	A	I	N	E	M	O	O	T
A	B	S	T	R	A	C	T	R	E	V	U	E
R	O	L	L	W	A	Y	E	L	A	P	S	E
T	A	M	A	L	E	M	O	N	G	R	E	L

28 FOR MEMBERS ONLY HINT

1-Across starts in the ninth square of the top row.

50 DIRTY WORDS HINT

1-Across starts in the tenth square of the top row.

76 MYSTERY LOVERS HINT

1-Across starts in the fifth square of the top row.

96 ABOUT FACE HINT

1-Across starts in the eighth square of the top row.

109 DOUBLE CROSS 11

A. REVENANT
B. OPPORTUNITY
C. GROSS TON
D. EVOCATIVE
E. RIVE
F. KINESCOPE
G. ACCESSORY
H. HASP
I. NOTION
J. HOROLOGY
K. OSSIA
L. WYOMING MASSACRE
M. TRAVERS
N. HALF A MIND
O. ENATION
P. WINGING IT
Q. EROS
R. ASWARM
S. TRIFLER
T. HEAVY-DUTY
U. ELIS
V. RAMOSE
W. WIND TUNNEL
X. ALAMO
Y. STRANGE BEDFELLOWS

As … media men say, TV makes every living room an arena. If that's what you want for your living room, televised sport can be thrilling. A good director shows aspects you cannot see on scene: lips moving in profanity, a winner's glower, a loser's tears.—Roger Kahn, *How the Weather Was*

112 DSZQUPHSBNT!

1. KEEP SMILING. When asked how to retain stiff upper lip in battle, flip colonel suggests extra dab of mustache wax.
2. BEAT IT! Marching to the sound of your own drummer is OK until you try for employment with a symphony.
3. HAIR APPARENT. Lady Godiva was smart. What taxman would risk husbandly wrath by seeking her hidden assets?
4. PLEASANT DREAMS. Tedious, vexatious exercises act as soporific. Insomniacs rely on cryptograms with warm milk.
5. BLOCKED SHOT. Filming picturesque mosque, camera buff rued ban against taking photo of exquisite odalisque.
6. BUILDING TENSION. Victorian architecture's curlicued scrollwork, gingerbread ornamentation give painters nightmares.
7. LANGUAGE BARRIER. English syntax perplexes exchange student struggling with irregular verbs, idiomatic expressions.
8. I AM THE GREATEST! Unblushing titleholder, fresh from boxing triumph, unknowingly bores friends through unending braggadocio.

110 SCHEDULE SCRAMBLE

The day lasts from 9 A.M. to 6 P.M., with an hour for lunch (clue 7) and 30 minutes traveling time (two 15-minute cab rides, from clue 8). This leaves 7½ hours for the eight meetings. Since only two meetings have the same duration, there are two possible sets of times, with either two 15-minute meetings or two 30-minute meetings. Given that the shortest meeting is in the morning, there cannot be two 15-minute meetings. The durations of the eight meetings, therefore, are 15, 30, 30, 45, 60, 75, 90, and 105 minutes.

The longest meeting, then, is 1 hour and 45 minutes long, and Mr. Eliot's before it is 45 minutes (clue 3). If these two meetings occur in the morning, along with the two cab rides and the shortest meeting, only 15 minutes are left over. Since there can be only one 15-minute meeting, the longest meeting must be in the afternoon. Of the 4½ hours of meetings in the afternoon, three hours are occupied by Mr. Eliot, the longest meeting, and one of the 30-minute meetings. The remaining meeting of the afternoon, then, is 90 minutes long.

The morning meetings, therefore, last 15, 30, 60, and 75 minutes. The longest meeting of the morning begins at 10:00 and ends at 11:15. Since the following meeting cannot begin at that time, the longest meeting must be the one at Washington's, with 15-minute cab rides before and after it. The trip to Washington's begins at 9:45, so it must be preceded by the 30- and 15-minute meetings, in that order. The hour-long meeting with Quay's (clue 2) must begin at 11:30.

The first meeting in the afternoon must be 30 or 90 minutes long; otherwise, the second meeting would begin at 15 minutes past the hour. If the second meeting of the afternoon is 30 or 90 minutes long, then the final meeting would begin at 4:15; therefore it must be the 45-minute meeting with Mr. Eliot. The third meeting, then, begins at 15 minutes before the hour, which means it must be with the woman from Taft's, not Ms. Bunyan. Ms. Bunyan's meeting, which must last longer than an hour (clue 2), must be the 90-minute meeting. Since the final meeting is with a man (clue 4), Ms. Bunyan's meeting must be the first in the afternoon, with the final meeting lasting 30 minutes.

Since Dickens arrives 2 hours before the person from Vare's (clue 9), his meeting must begin at 11:30. Therefore Dickens is from Quay's and Ms. Bunyan is from Vare's. By elimination, the woman from Sherman's arrives at 9:30, after the meeting with Ms. Golding at 9:00 (clue 1). Since Ms. Hardy cannot be in the next meeting after Ms. Golding (because their initials are alphabetically adjacent), she must be in the 3:45 meeting, with Taft's. Since Fielding cannot be after Ms. Golding, the 9:30 meeting must be with Ms. Chaucer. Mr. Arnold is not from Underwood's, so he must be from Washington's in the 10:00 meeting. Since Polk's is before Reed's (clue 5), it must be at 9:00, with Mr. Eliot from Reed's at 3:00.

In summary:

9:00-9:30	Ms. Golding	Polk's
9:30-9:45	Ms. Chaucer	Sherman's
10:00-11:15	Mr. Arnold	Washington's
11:30-12:30	Mr. Dickens	Quay's
12:30-1:30	LUNCH	
1:30-3:00	Ms. Bunyan	Vare's
3:00-3:45	Mr. Eliot	Reed's
3:45-5:30	Ms. Hardy	Taft's
5:30-6:00	Mr. Fielding	Underwood's

113 500 RUMMY

C A R A M E L							
8 8 8 8 2 3 4							41
C A R A W A Y							
8 8 8 8 2 3 4							41
C L O S E S T							
9 10 J Q A A A							42
C L O S E T S							
9 10 J Q A A A							42
C L O T H E S							
9 10 J A A A A							33
E C H E L O N							
9 9 9 3 4 5 6							45
E M B A R G O							
A 2 3 4 J J J							40
E M B R Y O S							
A 2 3 5 5 5 5							26
E N S U R E D							
Q Q Q 8 9 10							67
G R O C E R Y							
J J J 2 3 4 5							44
I N S P I R E							
K K K 10 J Q							70

K I N D R E D							
6 6 6 7 8 9 10							52
L E C H E R Y							
9 9 9 9 3 4 5							48
M E L O D I C							
2 3 4 5 10 10 10							44
R E S I D U E							
J Q K 7 7 7 7							58
S O R C E R Y							
5 5 5 2 3 4 5							29
S Q U A L I D							
5 6 7 8 10 10 10							56
S Q U A L O R							
5 6 7 8 J J J							56
S Q U E L C H							
5 6 7 9 9 9 9							54
U N E Q U A L							
Q Q Q 6 7 8 9							60
W A Y S I D E							
2 3 4 5 7 7 7							35
Total Score							983